Build Your Team
Build Your Dream

*Your Blueprint for Success
in Network Marketing*

Dave Bradley
Rodney Brandt

Foreword by Julie Ziglar Norman

WCC Press

Writing Career Coach Press (a division of Writing Career Coach, 14665 Fike Rd., Riga, MI 49276) functions only as book publisher. As such, the ultimate design, content, editorial accuracy, and views expressed or implied in this work are those of the authors.

ISBN 13: 978-1-938283-02-4

ISBN 10: 1938283023

Contents

Foreword

I believe Dave Bradley and Rodney Brandt have written THE book on Network Marketing! If you are fortunate enough to own a copy of *Build Your Team, Build Your Dream: Your Blueprint for Success in Network Marketing*, you have all the information you need to build a solid, profitable business.

Network Marketing has had an incredibly positive influence in my family's life. My father, motivational icon Zig Ziglar, got his start in direct sales, fell in love with Network Marketing and ultimately ended up motivating and inspiring countless individuals to believe in themselves, to understand that they already had the qualities and character traits they needed to build a business of their own and take responsibility for their life and livelihood. Dave Bradley and Rodney Brandt have managed to take their training to the next level. In my opinion, this book is the most complete, concise, enlightening directive ever written on how to successfully, systematically, build a Network Marketing business. It also happens to be the most entertaining read I've ever seen on what can spiral downward into terribly dry subject matter. I enjoyed every story and every example that was used to breathe refreshing life into material that is traditionally subjected to the "how to" format.

When two men with a foundation of strong ethical leadership and decades of personal Network Marketing experience join forces to write a book like this you can expect life-changing, life-building information! You'll learn what it takes on a personal level to jump into the world of entrepreneurism. You will discover how to move from where you are to becoming a nonconformist visionary with the potential to earn an income beyond what most dare to imagine. You'll become a builder of people and your Dream will take on new meaning as you see the lives of team members you've come to respect and love changed for the better.

Over the years, Network Marketing has provided our family lifelong friends, motivation and inspiration, income, business connections and opportunities, and access to superior products and services. If I had had this book, this blueprint, when I got involved in my first Network Marketing venture I could have saved myself months of trial and error. I would never have become as disorganized as I was and I would have been able to build, educate, and stay in touch with my team with just a fraction of the personal effort I expended.

If I were told I could only have one Network Marketing tool, I would choose the best tool available today—Dave Bradley and Rodney Brandt's *Build Your Team, Build Your Dream: Your Blueprint for Success in Network Marketing.*

Julie Ziglar Norman
Founder of Ziglar Women
International Inspirational Speaker
Author of *Growing Up Ziglar: A Daughter's Broken Journey from Heartache to Hope*

Introduction

Take an honest look at your life: Is it everything you dreamed it would be? Do you have what you want or have you settled for what you have?

If we were to ask every person on the earth whether or not they believe they can have their Dream Life, we are quite certain the majority would say, "I wish I could...but I don't believe I can. I think I can have a good life, but not a Dream Life."

It's sad that people think this, because it is absolutely not true. You *can* have your Dream Life. And, we want you to have it!

We entitled this book *Build Your Team, Build Your Dream* for multiple reasons. First, it takes a team to win in this business; you cannot do this on your own. By building a network, you are able to multiply your time and effort through leveraging the time and effort of others. That's the formula for having both financial and time freedom.

In addition to building a team, you must *build the people on the team*. This means you must be a skilled leader, mentor and encourager. You have to be other-people focused, putting their needs ahead of yours. It's not about using people to build your business; it's about using your business to build people.

If you build a team and build the people on the team, you will build your Dream. If you care for their Dream, *your* Dream will care for itself. To build a team, you will need to become highly skilled at working with people. You need to know how people think, why they say what they say and do what they do.

We're going to show you not only what to say and do in your business, but also what *not* to say and do. You will see a lot of dialogue in this book. Many of the concepts and teaching points are modeled through conversations and role-playing.

This book gives you the wisdom, business principles and practical knowledge—even some tough love—that has served us well in our more than 30 years of combined network marketing experience. You will also benefit from the insights and experiences of several other network marketers whose stories appear in this book.

There is a lot of material in these pages, so we suggest you read it in small chunks. There are several topics in each chapter. Try reading two or three of these at a time and then spend a while thinking about how to incorporate them into your business. Be sure also to utilize the exercises at the end of each chapter and bounce ideas and questions off your upline.

The book begins with a call for you to become a dreamer. The middle section is the "how to" and is followed by a return to your Dream. There is a great deal of significance in the fact that the book begins and ends with your Dream.

After you have read *Build Your Team, Build Your Dream,* you may realize that you are not yet where you need to be. But you also won't be where you used to be. Best of all...you'll be reaping the benefits of having made this Blueprint for Success in Network Marketing your own!

Sincerely,
Dave Bradley & Rodney Brandt

P.S. There are numerous titles used in network marketing, among them distributor, independent business owner, consultant and representative. For purposes of this book, we will use the terms "networker" and "network marketer" to refer to anyone who operates a network marketing business. Also, our use of the term "network marketing" includes businesses that might also be described as "direct sales."

ONE

Why

Do you have a Dream? If so, what is it? What if you never had to work for money another day in your life?

What if you had the money...

and the time...

to go anywhere...

and do anything...

for any reason?

What would you do?

Maybe you would buy a larger house; maybe *several* houses. You might spend more time with your family. Perhaps you would travel. (Haven't you always wanted to see the world?) You could volunteer your time and give large sums of money to charitable causes.

Do you think about those things? When is the last time you allowed a Dream to run unbridled over the landscape of your mind, no saddle on your back, no bit in your mouth, nothing holding you back? You, completely free, imagining yourself doing things you'd love to do, but wonder if you ever will.

We are going to challenge you to follow your imagination, to open your mind to what's possible. You really *can* have more in this life. You really *can* have what you want.

But, it starts with *knowing* what you want. You need to be clear about why you are in this business, what you hope to get out of it. That shouldn't be too difficult, right? After all, don't we all already know that?

The answer, unfortunately, is: no, most people *don't* know. A surprising number of us—we're willing to bet it's a majority—have no clear idea why we joined network marketing. In fact, we've never even taken the time to seriously think about it.

Why We Don't Dream

Think back to the lazy, endless summer days of your youth: no school, no homework; the only worry on your mind whether or not the fish were biting that day or finding enough other kids in the neighborhood for a good ball game.

Lying on our backs, digging our toes into the grass and gazing up at clouds floating lazily across the sky, we would boast to each other about the amazing things we would do some day.

Did you dream of being a princess? A cowboy? A fireman? Perhaps you were certain that one day you would compete in the Olympics or fly to the moon.

Granted, most of our childhood dreams were unrealistic; not many girls actually grow up to be a princess. But, does that really matter? Isn't the most important thing that we dared to dream at all? When we're kids, the significance of our dreams is not in the dream, but in the dreaming. It's in allowing ourselves to imagine a better future, whatever that future might be.

Just A Paycheck

In the Oscar-nominated movie *Up In The Air*, George Clooney plays the part of Ryan Bingham, a corporate downsizing specialist. Companies that are about to eliminate employees hire Bingham's firm to do the firing for them. In one of the film's many poignant scenes, Bingham is looking at the resume of the person he is letting go and notices that the man studied French culinary cuisine while in college. Yet, he took a corporate office job following graduation.

"How much did they first pay you to give up on your dreams?" Bingham asks him. "And, when were you going to stop and come back and do what makes you happy?"[1]

A man losing his job is a sad story. Even more sad is giving up our dreams for a job we don't really like but settle for because it pays the bills.

Think about what you currently do for a living. If someone asked you why you do it, how would you answer? Would you be able to give an affirmative reason? You might say, "I've wanted to do this since I was a little girl" or "I'm drawn to this; I love doing it!"

Or, would you cite a reason that reflects chance more than purpose? "This is the job I got out of high school and I've just been here ever since," "I joined the family business because it seemed like the thing to do," or "I applied here because it was a good way to make money."

So many of us start down a particular career path because a job becomes available and it seems like the best option (or the only option). Someone may even recommend it to us and tell us we'd be good at it. So, we take it.

Before we know it, we've got rent and a car payment. Then we get married and have a second car payment and a mortgage on top of that. Along come children and more responsibility and then a bigger house.

Our job—sure, it was fun for a while—becomes a grind. It's just a paycheck. What we do for a living no longer inspires us; it doesn't challenge us. We become bored at work and have to fight the urge to goof off. We don't give our best effort to our employer and then rationalize our poor work ethic: *They don't pay me enough, anyway.* At home, we're anxious and irritable. We come to hate Mondays.

THE CORPORATE TRAP

Not all of us wind up in our vocation by accident. Some of us have purposely invested a lot of time, money and effort into our education and training, all to pursue a career or business we truly enjoy.

But, even when we love what we do it's easy to become disillusioned. In the corporate world, we have to deal with office politics, unfair work schedules, getting passed over for promotions and rarely being paid what we think we deserve.

We get sucked into climbing the corporate ladder. We're willing to work long hours and live our life out of a suitcase while our family stays at home just to move ourselves up a rung or two. We eat on the run and neglect our health and skip vacations, because, well, that's what you have to do to get ahead.

If we're not careful, our position on the ladder becomes our identity. Our professional ego wants to make it about the title and the corner office and the status we *think* that gives us. We're more concerned with how we look on the corporate ladder than where the ladder is taking us. As author Stephen Covey puts it, "It's incredibly easy to get caught up in an activity trap, in the busy-ness of life, to work harder at climbing the ladder of success only to discover it's leaning against the wrong wall."[2]

Think about that for a minute. When is the last time you looked closely at the wall *your* ladder is leaning against? What are you working so hard at? What are you giving your life to? Do you feel good about the company you work for or the business you're in? Does your job allow ample time for you to be with your family and pursue your hobbies? Do you still love your work?

Fifty percent of employees hate their jobs, either because of their company's pay and promotion structure or because they simply no longer like what they do.[3,4] There is a very good chance that you are among them.

Understand that as long as you are employed for someone else, it doesn't matter how hard you work to climb the ladder; it will never be under your control and it will always be against someone else's wall. You are building *their* dream, not yours. There is no guarantee that you can keep your spot on the ladder; you could be kicked off at any time. Furthermore, as long as you remain on the corporate ladder, you will always be looking at the rear end of the person directly above you!

We are not suggesting that you quit your job, or that working for someone else is a bad idea *if you are happy with your life.* If you are encouraged by the path you are on, fantastic! We congratulate you.

However, the fact that you are reading this book suggests that maybe—just maybe—your inner voice is saying, "There's got to be more to life than this."

MOVING YOUR LADDER

Like the guy who once had a vision of working in the culinary arts, we lose our ability to dream. As we get older, we think about our Dream less and less until one day we no longer think of it at all. We stop dreaming. Worse yet, we don't even *realize* that we've stopped dreaming.

We have the cars and the nice house, the flat screen television and the latest electronic gadgets. We eat out and buy new clothes whenever we feel like it. We come home from work, plop down on the couch, turn the TV on and our brains off. We call this the Good Life.

Whether we realize it or not, we're trapped. We're trapped in a job we don't particularly like but can't quit because we have to finance this life we've built. We have everything we need to be comfortable, but we're not happy. We're restless.

We could change jobs. That might give us a change of scenery for a bit or bring us more money. But, where has the money got us thus far? More money doesn't change the fact that something is missing. Our lives have a void, and we can't quite put our finger on it.

Have you considered that the angst inside you might be a call to move your ladder? What if you could move your ladder to your own wall? What if you could have a business where *you* determine how much you earn, *you* determine how high you can climb, *you* decide where you put your efforts and when? What if you could create your future instead of letting someone else dictate it?

Now, imagine helping other people move their ladders to *their* own wall. Imagine that by doing that, by helping others get what *they* want, you would get what *you* want.

Defining Your Why

Not long after you joined your network marketing company, someone in your upline probably asked you to define your WHY. (If no one did, they should have.) Defining your WHY should be one of the first things you do.

Your WHY is your inspiration, your main goal. It's the whole point of starting your business. It's the reason you are willing to try something you've never done before, step way outside your comfort zone and face your fears.

When Doris Leissing started her network marketing business, there was no doubt about *her* Why. She had an immediate need and it was a big one:

> My husband and I faced a real dilemma. He had pioneered a church in the North Carolina mountains and I had elected to set aside my nursing career and focus on home schooling my children, caring for my elderly mother, and helping my husband in the ministry. As he neared retirement age we found ourselves in a precarious financial situation. Since he had entered ministry late in life we had no savings, owned no home, and had no security.
>
> We began to pray for some kind of financial breakthrough when the invitation came to look into a network marketing company. Initially, we were both very hesitant. I, in particular, had a negative attitude toward that industry. I had never sold anything in my life and couldn't see myself doing it. We were impressed, however, with the quality of the people we met, the products and the compensation plan of that company. Our early experiences were surprisingly positive.
>
> As our family began to have positive experiences with the products, our business began to expand into several states. After my husband died unexpectedly, just a year and a half into our new business, I became the sole support of my mother, my daughter and myself, and the primary business builder in our new venture.

You may have a similar situation, a financial emergency of some kind. It may be the result of losing your job. Perhaps, you or someone in your family has a serious health issue and medical expenses have left you near bankruptcy. Maybe you are at retirement age and realize you aren't financially prepared. In these cases, there is little ambiguity regarding your Why; it is very much in your face.

However, most people who join this industry have no emergency, no urgent problem. Let's assume that you are doing okay, financially. You might even be well off, living comfortably. Then again, maybe you aren't swimming in money, but the bills are being paid and you're even putting a little away each month. In either case, money is not a problem. Everyone in the family is relatively healthy and has a good outlook. Overall, life isn't bad. In fact, it's pretty good.

With no pressing issue in your life, you can't be exactly sure why you joined network marketing, but something drew you in. Perhaps your decision wasn't the result of deliberately thinking things through, but more of a sense or a feeling. It just *felt* right.

From the start, you asked a lot of questions about how you should do this business; but, you never really asked *why* you should do it. Probably, that's because the "how" question is one we ask of other people while the "why" question is one we must ask of ourselves. And, we're not very good at asking ourselves questions. Introspection isn't something most of us do very often or very well.

So, when someone first asked you what you hoped to get out of this business, how did you respond? Did you give a thorough and thoughtful answer? Or, did a blank look come over your face, like a deer in headlights? You may have managed to stammer out something like, "Uh, I don't know; to make money, I guess."

Well, making money is important. That's what separates a business from a hobby or volunteer program. But that's not really your WHY. If things are going pretty well in your life, you obviously have a source of income. So, if you are already making money, that really can't be your reason for joining network marketing, can it?

Here's another common response: "I just want to help people." Okay, that's great. Helping people is good; most of us really want to do that. But like the answer "I want to make money," wanting to help people doesn't really address why someone would join this business.

You might disagree with that. "It most certainly *does* answer the question for me!" you protest. "My company's products are life-changing! I'm in this because I want to help people with these products."

Well, let's look at that more closely. (By the way, we believe you when you say your company's products are life-changing. Many of the best products in the world are distributed through network marketing.) Let's say you have a health product that helps people address medical problems or prevent future problems. Maybe your company's products help people look better and give them a healthier self-esteem. Or, perhaps your products protect people in some way or give them peace of mind. It may have been great products that initially attracted you to this business and now you are passionate about sharing them with others.

But, when it comes to answering the WHY question, wanting to help people—life changing product or not—is no better an answer than wanting to make money. Why? Because neither answer goes deep enough.

If you want to make money, there are easier ways to do it than starting a business, something most of us have never done before. If you want to help people, there are ways to do it much less difficult than network marketing. You might volunteer at a nursing home, your child's school or a homeless shelter. And by the way, if all you want to do is help people, does that mean you are willing to give back the profits your company is paying you? Probably not.

Why are we making such a big deal of this? Because it *is* a big deal. It's HUGE! Making money and helping people are simply top-of-mind responses to a very deep and very important question. You absolutely *must* know your WHY, and in most cases you will have to drill far below the surface to find it.

Drilling Down

If you need some help determining your WHY, we have an exercise that will help. Start by asking yourself: "Why am I in this business?" Whatever your answer is to that question, ask yourself: "Why is that important?" Continue to ask yourself "Why is that important" until you have a clear answer.

Here's an example:

Why am I in this business?

Because I need to do something different with my life.

Why is that important?

Because I work too many hours.

Why is THAT important?

Because my kids rarely see me.

Why is THAT important?

Because I want to be part of their lives.

Why is THAT important?

Because I love them. I want to know them and want them to know me. Because the values I model for them are most likely the values they will adopt for themselves.

Why is THAT important?

Because I believe that what our children become is a direct result of the time we invest in them. And, I want them to grow up to be good people so they might enjoy life and make the world a better place.

Next, look what happens when you put all of those responses into one statement:

> I work too many hours and I don't see my children nearly enough. I need a way to make money that will allow me to spend more time with them. I want to know who they are and for them to know me. I want to model for them my values in the hope that they will adopt these values for themselves, because I believe that what our children become is a direct result of the time we invest in them. I want my children to grow up to be good so that they might enjoy life and make the world a better place. That is why I am in this business.

Now, *that* is clear. THAT is powerful. Compare that statement to "I want to make money" or "I just want to help people." Do you see the difference?

When you dare to ask yourself probing questions, when you drill down far below the surface, things begin to come into focus. Your WHY ceases to be this fuzzy, vague notion that produces a blank look on your face. Instead, you know what you want. And, as we have already told you, knowing what you want is the first step toward getting it.

Your Dream Partner

It is very important that you have a partner who supports you and your Dream. For most of us, this will be our spouse or significant other. It might also be our parents, a close friend or in many cases, our upline. Your Dream Partner is your encourager, your cheerleader. They are invested in your Dream; they're in your corner. They are the ones who believe in you even when you don't believe in yourself.

Early in her business, Donna Reid-Mitchell discovered just how important having such an encourager is. Donna was born in Jamaica and in 2001 emigrated with her family to The United States. Today, she is a representative for a cosmetics and beauty company and makes her home in Frisco, Texas. All it took was an encouraging word to light a fire in her:

> I was living in New York at the time and I had just had a new baby. She was three months old and I was not ready to put her into daycare and go back to working full-time. I wanted to have a business that would help me generate a little money. I did not want to have to ask my husband each time I needed some. I just wanted some pocket change.
>
> Six months after I started my business, I became a single mother with two children. I needed to make enough money to take care of myself and them, so I went back to work full-time as a hair stylist. I was doing pretty well with that. But, I was on my own and living in New York is expensive. And, having gone through the separation, I was at a low point emotionally. It was all very hard.
>
> One day when I was complaining about not having enough money, my seven-year-old son said, "Mommy, why don't you do more with your business?" He said, "You're the best business lady I know. If you do more, I will help you." When he said that, I thought "Whoa! If he believes in me that much, then okay we are going to do it." I started to dream bigger and to work harder at my business. Just having someone believe in me more than I believed in myself...I can truly say that was the pivotal point in my career.

As you listened to Donna's story, could you relate? Picture in your mind that little boy saying, "Mommy, you're the best." Do you think that inspired her? You bet it did! She said herself that it was the turning point in her business.

Donna was a single mom who had bills to pay. It's why she went back to work. Given her situation, it's not surprising that her business had been pretty much an afterthought; she had her hands full just trying to be a provider and a mom. But, when another person partnered with her in her Dream—*Mommy, you're the best. If you do more, I will help you*—it changed everything. Those words infused life into her Dream. It's amazing what can happen when just one other person believes in us.

Within 20 months, Donna's business was generating $4 million in annual revenue. In one 90-day period, she developed so many new business builders in her group she set a company record. Today, Donna has more than 3,000 representatives in her organization and makes a very comfortable six-figure income. She now uses her experience to teach others:

> I have never forgotten those words from my son and how important they were to me. I try to instill the belief in my teams even when they doubt that they can be one of our company's best.
>
> I also try to instill in them that it's very important to partner with people who have bigger dreams and goals than you do. And, for me that is my children. When I say I want a new house, they want me to get a house on a two-acre property whereas I would be comfortable with a nice little two-story house. When I want to take a vacation, I'm thinking Hawaii; they're thinking Europe, they're thinking Africa.
>
> They're the ones that keep me waking up at 6 a.m. every morning working my business. They keep me stretching myself and I absolutely love that.

Two Paths

At this point, some clarification might be helpful. We've established that each of us joins network marketing for a reason and that reason is commonly referred to as our WHY. We discussed how some of us have a very obvious WHY but a majority of us can't really put a finger on it.

To understand this better, think of your WHY branching off in one of two directions. One path follows an urgent problem in your life; we'll call that path a Need. The second path doesn't follow a Need, but instead leads to *that thing* we know we want but struggle to describe. This second path is most certainly there, but is one we don't clearly see until we start drilling down into our life. This path is our Dream (see Fig. 1.1).

The Dream path leads to that wonderful place where money and time are no longer a concern to you. This is the place where you truly can do anything you want, at any time you want, anywhere you want, for any reason you want. It's waking up every morning knowing that what you do that day is absolutely, completely up to you.

It's where you don't have to imagine what life could be like someday because you are living it—living The Dream.

Fig. 1.1

WHY

Need   Dream

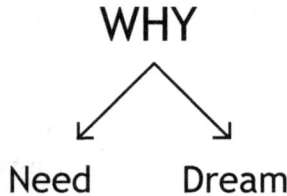

Why Your Why Is So Important

Moving your ladder is not easy. It is heavy and unwieldy. You will have to work hard and you will have to develop a thick skin. Your resolve will be tested many times. Circumstances will come against you. People will come against you.

But you have something that most people do not have: you have a WHY. It doesn't matter whether your WHY is an urgent Need or that big Dream deep inside you. What matters is that you have it. When you have a WHY you have focus, you have acceleration and you have strength.

YOUR COMPASS

Defining your WHY gives your business direction; it is your compass. When you were a kid and went on a school trip or a vacation with your parents, you had a destination. You were going someplace specific: a favorite camp ground or resort, a national park or monument or other place of historical significance.

Your parents or chaperones mapped out in advance the best route to take so that all of you could get there safely and in the shortest amount of time. It was deliberate and well defined.

Along the way, you asked a thousand times, "How long 'til we get there?" You were brimming with anticipation. You imagined what you would do when you arrived and chattered excitedly about it, as did everyone else on the trip.

Imagine, instead, that when you got into the car, climbed onto the bus or boarded your plane, that you had nowhere in particular to go. You were just going to see what happened, where things might lead.

That would have changed the trip dramatically. How could you envision all the things you would do and the fun you would have if you didn't know where you were going? What would happen to your excitement? It would probably turn to anxiety over not knowing where you would end up. What if you arrived somewhere only to discover you didn't like it?

Your business is also a trip of sorts, more like a journey. Defining your WHY at the outset is the act of giving that journey focus, a destination, a purpose. In the example we gave you earlier, it is the parent who is focused on finding a source of income that allows her to be at work less and at home more, so that she can invest in her children. That is how your WHY serves as your compass; it is in knowing where you want to go.

THE WIND IN YOUR SAILS

Think about when you first started dating your husband, wife or significant other. Early in the relationship, sparks were flying. At times, it took your breath away. Your closest friends were the first ones to spot it. You didn't even have to tell them because it was obvious: you were in love! It was written all over your face, it was in the little things you said, even in the way you walked.

Your new love was on your mind day and night. Suddenly, the sun was brighter, the grass was greener and those little things that always annoyed you no longer mattered. Your sails were up and the wind was at your back!

It's the same in this business. When you connect to your Dream, things change. Sparks fly as you think about the possibilities, how much different your life can be. You have that excitement and energy you did as a child. You can hardly wait to share your business opportunity with the next person.

Your friends see it on your face, in the little things you say and in the way you walk. (Don't be surprised if they want to know if you're in love!) Even people who don't know you take notice. They say to themselves, "There's something about her I really like." It's because you have the wind at your back. They may not see it, but they definitely feel it. And, so do you.

Your Anchor

In marriage, the beginning is always heavy on romance. But, eventually the honeymoon ends. The pressures of life creep in. Difficulties arise. We have differences of opinion and we let each other down. There are days when we feel like we don't even love our spouse. The romance comes and goes. But, for the marriage to survive, true love and commitment must remain.

It is no different in your business. There will be trials. You will get mad. You will get frustrated. There will be days that you don't want to work your business, days when you aren't even sure if you still *like* your business.

But, you don't leave your marriage and you don't abandon your business because of a momentary feeling. When couples are having marital problems, one of the best things they can do is go back to the time they met and reaffirm for each other all the reasons they fell in love, what they saw in the other person that made them want to build a life together. The trials of life may toss them back and forth, but if their relationship is anchored in true love it can withstand the storms.

You, too, must hold onto your Dream when these days come to your business. Your Dream is your anchor. Don't lose sight of it. Don't let it get away from you. When you start to get tossed about, reaffirm what led you to start your business. Tell yourself, "I don't care if it gets hard. I don't care if I feel like giving up. This is my Dream and I'm not letting go of it!"

The Right Vehicle

Whether you have a Dream or just want an answer to an urgent Need, network marketing can undoubtedly help you get it. But, it is far from your only option. If you need extra money, you could get a second job or a higher-paying job. If you love your craft but don't particularly like being an employee, you might start your own business. Do what you love to do, but work for yourself instead of someone else.

Perhaps you already have your own business, but have discovered that your business really owns *you*. True, you get to call the shots but you feel more like a glorified employee than a business owner.

Regardless of whether you are an employee or entrepreneur, you need to ask yourself this question: Can I achieve my Dream by continuing to do what I am doing now? Well, *can you?* Is your job or business going to deliver your Dream? Fear will try to keep you from addressing that question. We urge you to be brutally honest with yourself. *Can you achieve your Dream doing what you're doing?* You might even get input from a friend or mentor. If your honest assessment is "yes" and the people you trust agree with that, then it is likely that your best option is to stay the course. Keep doing what you're doing.

But if you can't answer "yes" to that question, then you need to ask yourself this one: "If I don't make a change now, how will my life be any different in five years? In 10 years?"

Ten years from now you will certainly be older, but will you be closer to your Dream? The reality is that only a very small percentage of people earn enough at their jobs or careers to achieve their Dream. The rest of us settle for a living. Our job may keep the Dream alive, but it will never deliver it. It's because our career choice simply cannot give us the combination of money and time freedom necessary to be free. The limit on our income and the fact that it takes most of our time to earn that income puts us in a box. As a result, we downsize our Dream to fit into that box.

What makes network marketing so appealing is that it has neither the limitations of a job nor a traditional business. Unlike working for someone else, you make all the decisions about your time and your income. Unlike a traditional business, which requires a lot of upfront money, managing employees and inventory, liability, insurance and who knows what else, network marketing is a simplified business model that can be done mostly with a telephone.

Let's assume you like your career and wouldn't dream of quitting your job. Perhaps you own a company and have no intention of ever selling it. Maybe you are self-employed in a profession that you love. No problem. Network marketing is a scalable business; you can work it in addition to what you are doing now. It will always meet you where you want to be.

Maybe you think you're too busy to add even one more thing to your life. Well, what other business allows you to leverage part-time hours into a full-time income? No other business model is better designed to fit your life. What other business can you put down for a time if necessary and pick up later? Try taking 12 months away from your traditional business and we'll see if it's still standing when you come back.

The arguments in support of network marketing are numerous. But the only person who can convince you is *you*. You have to sell yourself.

We've already given you several things to consider, but here is the most important one: Do you believe that network marketing is the right vehicle to take you to your Dream? We urge you to give that some serious thought. Ask yourself: *Do I believe that network marketing is the right vehicle to take me to my Dream?*

You might be thinking "Maybe," "I think so" or "I hope so." If you are relatively new to network marketing, then any of those answers is okay...for now. But, you need to know for sure as soon as possible, through learning about the business and learning about yourself. The balance of this book gives you that opportunity.

Are you ready?

Quick Review: Why

1) The first thing you must do is define your WHY.
2) Defining your WHY will require you to search deeply within yourself.
3) You need a Dream Partner, someone who believes in you and will encourage you.
4) Your WHY will be either an urgent Need or a Big Dream.
5) Your WHY will be your guide and will keep you going when things get difficult.
6) You must determine if network marketing is the right vehicle for you to reach your Dream.

Exercise

1) In the space below, write your WHY. Your WHY may be an immediate Need or it might be your ultimate Dream. Whichever it is, write it down. Include your spouse or significant other in this process.

2) Is network marketing the best way for you to achieve your WHY, or is there a better option available to you? Once you have determined which way is best for you, write down the reasons it is better than your other options.

TWO

How Network Marketing Works

Before we proceed, we should acknowledge that although the basic principles of network marketing are clear and universal, how they are put into practice can vary. The way you have been taught to do the business and the way you are teaching others may be much different from the next network marketer. There will be differences from company to company, even differences among groups within the same company.

If any of the teachings in this book are contrary to what you have learned from your training and experience, we advise you to discuss this with the people who are mentoring you. The last thing we want is to create any confusion or contention. Rather, we hope that the knowledge and wisdom shared here will be a resource that launches your business to new heights!

Network marketing is a simple business, but it is not easy. It takes hard work, skill and persistence. But, it's worth it! We are going to lay out a step-by-step process for you, one that will put you in position to build a solid and dynamic business.

The Industry

Let's start with an explanation of the business model. Network marketing is a distribution method, a way to bring products and services to the marketplace. Let's say you own a company that manufactures water guns. For your company to be profitable, you need a way to get those water guns into the hands of consumers.

One way to do that is to set up retail stores around the country and hire a sales staff. You would have to pay rent and utilities for the building, transportation costs to get the product from your manufacturing plant to the retail outlets, office supplies for each outlet, wages and benefits for your staff and advertising among other things. You could also sell your water guns to existing retail stores, which would eliminate much of your costs but in return you would have to give the retail stores much of your profit.

Another option exists for you and that is to distribute your water guns through *a network of independent marketers.* And, that is exactly what the network marketing model is: independent business owners who do not have retail stores, but instead market the product on a one-to-one basis directly with the consumer. You will have to share your profits with the network marketers who distribute your product, just as you would with the retail stores. But, an additional advantage of network marketing is that you don't need to advertise your products, because your marketers are doing it for you on a word-of-mouth basis. They personally demonstrate to your consumers how your water guns provide children and adults alike a safe and fun form of recreation!

For products sold in retail stores, as much as 80 percent of what the customer pays is consumed by the cost of manufacturing the product, advertising, employee compensation and distribution costs. The company keeps the rest as profit. For companies that use the network marketing method of distribution, the costs are similar: roughly 80 percent of the gross revenue. However, instead of paying wages and benefits to a sales force and spending money on traditional advertising, the company pays commissions to independent marketers to advertise and distribute its products.

Trends

Cosmetics, personal care and wellness products account for nearly 60 percent of all products sold through network marketing.[1] However, the industry has proven adaptable to a very diverse product line. Many common items in your home are now distributed through network marketing, including clothing, books and toys, food and household items, appliances and even utilities.

As the number of goods and services has grown over the years, so has the industry. In the 10-year period from 2000 to 2009, network marketing retail sales grew 43 percent worldwide, with the global sales force increasing 91 percent during that same period.[2] Today, nearly 88 million network marketers around the world sell more than $132 billion in products and services annually.[3] Eight in 10 people work their business part-time and 3 in 4 are women. [4]

The emergence of personal computers and the Internet has made network marketing even more attractive, as orders can be placed online by customers at their convenience and without the need for the network marketer to be involved. Computerization has also enhanced the speed of the enrollment process and the distribution of products and services. One can surmise that future advances in communication and information technologies will make the borderless network marketing industry even better.

Proponents of network marketing include business and investment moguls Warren Buffet, Robert Kiyosaki and Donald Trump, legendary motivator and performance trainer Zig Ziglar and *Success Magazine,* which calls network marketing "a proven system for success."[5]

Structure

Like the corporate world, network marketing has a pyramidal structure. In the corporate world, there is a president or CEO at the top and below her or him are vice-presidents. Each vice-president is in charge of a division of the company, such as manufacturing, warehousing, transportation, marketing, finance and human resources. Each of these vice-presidents may have several managers working under them, and each manager in turn will have supervisors. Finally, at the bottom are the entry level employees, often referred to as "line staff." The largest group of people is at the bottom of the pyramid. With each higher level there are fewer people and at the very top there is just one (see Fig. 2.1).

The structure is similar in network marketing. It begins with one person "sponsoring" another into the business. However, no one reports to another person; everyone is independent. Nor does anyone work for the company; they are each in business for themselves.

Let's say that you are sponsored into a network marketing business by your friend, Jane. Jane then brings Tom into the business. If you and

Tom each sponsor new people and this duplication continues, the structure takes on the shape of a pyramid (see Fig. 2.2). Jane also has a sponsor and her sponsor has a sponsor and so on. These people form an upward line away from you and are called your "upline." They are responsible for teaching and mentoring you.

Conversely, the people that you sponsor directly and the people they sponsor and so on form a downward line away from you and are called your "downline." (A downline is also referred to as a "leg," "group" or "organization.") You are responsible for teaching and mentoring your downline, with help from your upline.

Fig. 2.1

Fig. 2.2

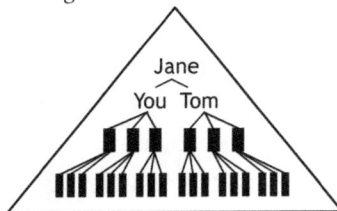

Pyramid Schemes

Network marketing has a pyramid structure; however, it is not a pyramid *scheme*. A pyramid scheme is an illegal system in which money is paid but there is no exchange of goods or services. Money is collected primarily for enrollment, a chance to "get into the game." Pyramid schemes are a form of fraud and illegal in many countries (including the United States).[6]

An example is what many call the "Airplane Game." To get a seat on the plane, you pay for a ticket. Let's say that ticket is $1,000. Once you have a seat, your goal is to recruit people to get on the plane after you—they, too, each pay $1,000 for a ticket—and when they do, this moves you toward the front of the plane where you collect on your investment. You start in Coach but as people get on behind you, you move into First Class, then to Crew, then to the cabin where you become Co-Captain and eventually Captain. Once you become Captain, you are next in line to exit the plane and collect your payday, which could be $8,000 or higher depending on the size of the plane.

The pyramid is not sustainable. It will eventually collapse when no more participants can be found—this is equivalent to the plane crashing—and many or all of those stuck on the plane will lose their "investment."

The Case for Network Marketing

The network marketing business model has an obvious appeal to the entrepreneur and we will address the reasons why shortly. But, did you know that companies and their customers enjoy many benefits, as well?

Companies that choose to distribute their products through network marketing do so for these reasons, among others:

1) They know that the most powerful form of advertising is one person telling another person about their experience using a particular product or service;
2) Network marketers can explain the unique features and benefits of a product in great detail, which is usually not possible through mainstream advertising;
3) Network marketers provide customer service after the sale, increasing customer loyalty;
4) Network marketers use the products themselves, further solidifying the company's market share;
5) Companies experience these additional benefits yet their marketing costs are no higher than if their products were retailed in stores;
6) It is very cost-efficient. Companies that choose traditional sales channels have to hire a sales staff and pay them wages, acquire a storefront and pay for expensive advertising campaigns all *before* the first product is sold. With network marketing, companies only pay out *after* the sale.

When products and services are retailed through the network marketing model, *consumers* benefit, too:

1) Most products sold through network marketing feature a money-back guarantee. This includes consumable products, which rarely have a money-back guarantee when purchased through traditional retail channels;

2) Customer service is typically better because the customer and distributor have a relationship;

3) Customers have the convenience of shopping from home; and

4) Customers have the option of receiving discounts on the products and earning an income by becoming a business partner.

The most powerful aspects of network marketing, however—and certainly the ones that are the most important to you—are the benefits it provides to the network marketer.

We will start by explaining how network marketing is not bound by the limitations of the traditional, bricks-and-mortar business model. First, your manufacturing plant can only produce water guns a maximum of 24 hours a day. You can produce them around the clock and hire a lot of people to keep the plant running constantly, but there are only so many hours in a day and it is impossible for you to exceed that limitation.

Second, you have only so much manufacturing capacity, only so much room for water gun assembly lines, only so much room for packaging and only so much room for your employees. You cannot exceed the physical boundaries of your manufacturing facility. So, you are limited also by space.

Leadership strategist Chris Widener says that these limitations result in "stationary income."[7] In other words, your business cannot grow beyond the physical limitations of time and space. True, you could expand your plant or build another one but in doing so you have significantly increased—perhaps doubled—your costs. You have to pay for more building, more permits, more raw materials, more employees, more packaging, more delivery trucks, and so on. It is a lot of effort, money and risk.

The network marketing business model, however, is not bound by the limitations of time and space. When you build a network, it works in various places and times simultaneously around the world. What if, as the owner of a water gun business, you could clone yourself and have hundreds—even thousands—of water gun businesses that didn't require you to be there to run each one? Wouldn't that be great? Well, that's how network marketing works!

It's called "duplication" and it is the key to having a solid and secure residual income. Imagine having a business that makes you money half way around the world while you are asleep in bed at night. Where else but network marketing can you shatter the time and space limits of a traditional business?!

If you are currently a traditional business owner, imagine having a business with these features:

- Extremely low start-up costs;
- Little to no ongoing costs;
- No fixed costs;
- No employee productivity issues;
- No large inventory;
- No geographical limitations;
- Portability;
- No debt.

If you are currently an employee and you spend your day working for someone else, imagine:

- Unlimited earning potential;
- A flexible schedule;
- Building your Dream, not someone else's;
- Security;
- No competing for promotions;
- No discrimination;
- No more trading time for money.

Regardless of whether you are a business owner or corporate employee, you can enjoy these additional benefits:

- Scalability;
- Residual income.

Low Start-Up Cost

If you were to start a traditional, bricks-and-mortar business you would have to make significant investments in things like product inventory, equipment, vehicles, benefits and wages, insurance, supplies, office furniture, computer hardware and software, a building lease or mortgage, utilities, building security, legal fees, professional fees, franchise fees, licenses, advertising, travel—the list goes on and on.

The cost to start a McDonald's restaurant is nearly $2 million.[8] That is the cost just to open the doors, before you sell even one hamburger! Of course, not everyone who starts a business turns to the king of fast food, but you get the idea that a traditional business comes at a significant cost.

For the small, independent business owner, start-up costs can be much less. The Wells Fargo/Gallup Small Business Index surveyed 604 small business owners nationwide and found their average start-up investment to be $10,000.[9] That's a far cry from $2 million for a McDonald's, but for most people it is still a prohibitive amount.

By contrast, most network marketing companies require an investment of less than $300. The absence of significant start-up costs opens the door to opportunity that would otherwise remain closed for the average person.

Few Ongoing Costs

Most businesses have many ongoing costs that are necessary to keep the business running. There are "overhead" costs which are not directly associated with producing a good or service and include things like rent, insurance, administrative costs and marketing. There are also ongoing costs that *are* directly associated with the production of goods and services, including wages and salaries, equipment and maintenance, and inventory.

The significance of ongoing costs is that a business does not make a profit until there are enough sales to cover these expenses. Companies know how much product they must sell each month just to break even.

Your network marketing business, however, has little to no ongoing costs. In most cases your customers can order directly from the parent company. The company absorbs the administrative costs of placing the order, pays all of the manufacturing and warehousing costs, handles all of the packaging and shipping, and even collects the payment from the customer. It is completely hands-free and cost-free for you.

No Fixed Costs

Many ongoing costs are "fixed," meaning they are constant month to month and have to be paid regardless of how many sales the business makes. Examples of fixed costs are rent, utilities, office supplies and salaries. Fixed costs can kill a business quickly. When sales are down and you are struggling to pay the bills, you likely won't find a sympathetic ear when you go to the building landlord and ask if you can skip that month's payment.

Everything you need for your network marketing business, on the other hand, is probably already in your home. Multi-million dollar businesses can be run with just a telephone, personal computer and an empty seat at the kitchen table!

NO EMPLOYEES

Almost every business owner who has employees will tell you that while they can help you have a profitable and enjoyable business, they can also be the source of lost productivity and myriad other problems. We can do our best to hire people we think are honest, hardworking and accountable, yet in a traditional business we will still have employees who are lazy, show up late or not at all, cause conflict and even steal from the company. The impact of bad employees goes far beyond lost profits; it can kill the morale of the entire company.

In network marketing, you have no employees. Because everyone is in business for themselves, the lazy network marketer hurts only himself. You don't need to worry about the people in your downline who don't show up for work. Just work with those who do!

NO LARGE INVENTORIES

Traditional businesses need to keep a large amount of their product on hand to fill customer orders. Since they do not know how many orders they will have in a given week, or even a given day, they must be prepared to meet an unknown demand. They do this by estimating the number of orders they will have and then storing or "warehousing" that amount of product. If the company not only distributes but also manufactures its products, it needs to warehouse the raw materials it uses. And, anywhere you have a need for warehousing, you have costs—the cost of the building, utilities, employees, security, and so on. A significant amount of a company's income cannot be used because it is invested right back into purchasing or creating more inventory.

In network marketing, you have none of those costs and very little (if any) of your money is tied up in inventory. You may need to carry a small inventory of your company's products, but mostly your customers and downline will order directly from the company. You do not have to make a continuous upfront investment in products that you then have to store. You don't have to worry about damaged products or expiration dates. You don't have the pressure of liquidating an inventory just to free up cash.

People place orders directly, you never touch the product and the company sends you a check. Better yet, they deposit your income directly into your bank account. What a deal!

NO GEOGRAPHICAL LIMITATIONS

Many business opportunities, particularly within the franchise model, limit you to doing business only in a certain area. You are assigned a territory and can look for customers only within those geographical boundaries. If you violate the territorial restriction, you risk being fined or losing your franchise or distributorship. This is done to protect the viability of each franchise, but it also serves to limit how big each franchise or distributorship can become.

In network marketing, there is no such restriction. You are free to build your business anywhere and everywhere your company operates. As a result, it is not unusual for a network marketer to have business in several countries around the world.

PORTABILITY

Network marketing is the ultimate portable, take-with-you-anywhere business. Since your business is essentially you, you can literally take it anywhere. If you go out of town to see relatives, you can do your business while you are gone. If you take a weekend to drive the kids back to college, you can take your business with you. If you want to live somewhere else, perhaps move to a nicer climate, you can take your business with you.

Try moving a manufacturing plant or an office building, or relocating your employees. Any traditional business owner who has had to do so will attest to the expense, aggravation and loss of productivity that go with it.

No Debt

With all of the start-up needs and operating costs that come with a traditional small business, it is not unusual for these businesses to carry large amounts of debt, especially in the first several years. Most traditional businesses do not turn a profit within their first three years and it is very much a hand-to-mouth existence. Even well-established businesses frequently take on debt, for things like new equipment or the renovation and expansion of their facilities.

Thankfully, network marketing requires none of this. You can be debt-free and profitable almost immediately without ever having to worry about servicing debt or having parts of your business repossessed or foreclosed on by a lender.

Earning Potential

As an employee, your earning potential is determined by your employer, generally in the form of a set salary or hourly wage. Commission-based jobs can offer unlimited pay, but often require you to share in office expenses and other costs. These jobs are also subject to the other limitations discussed below. How much you can earn is also impacted by how much the person above you makes. It is extremely rare for you to earn more than the person to whom you report.

As a network marketer, however, you enjoy unlimited earning potential. There is no cap on how much you can make. The larger your network becomes, the more you earn. And, because the business rewards you appropriately for your level of effort and skill, it is not unusual for network marketers to earn more than their sponsor and others in their upline. This is an important distinction between network marketing, which is a legitimate business model, and pyramid schemes which are unethical and illegal.

Flexibility

If you have a job, you are generally told when you have to be at work and how long you have to stay. You may even have rigid break times. You have to have vacation time and personal days approved in advance. If you have a job where you are "on call," it can be hard to plan anything in your life. How many of your kids' recitals and ball games have you missed because they happened while you were at work? How many times have you used your lunch hour for a dental appointment? How many times have you looked out your office window on a beautiful day and wished you could go for a walk or play a round of golf?

In network marketing, you plan your work around your life, not your life around your work. You still have to be disciplined and at times work long hours, but you have flexibility in determining how and when you do the work.

Build Your Own Dream

As an employee in the corporate world, the investment you make in your company has a limited return: it is limited to what they decide to pay you, and that pay stops the day you stop working. Your efforts are building someone else's Dream, not yours. You are working for something you will never own.

There is also the matter of your professional development. Companies often make considerable investment in training their employees. However, most of that training is geared toward making you more skilled at your job or more motivated to do your job. Such training, by and large, is not about helping you advance to the top of the corporate ladder.

Also in the mix is the supervisor-employee dynamic. Generally speaking, it is not in your supervisor's best interest to supply you with knowledge, skills and wisdom equal to that which she has acquired. Doing so would make her replaceable, and so she has a vested interest in limiting your professional development. It is a survival tactic.

The nature of the corporate world is overwhelmingly "Win-Lose." For every person who wins there is a loser. For every person who gets the promotion, there is at least one who did not. For this reason, the higher up the corporate ladder you go the more treacherous the climb becomes.

Conversely, a spirit of teamwork permeates a strong network marketing organization. It is in the best interest of a sponsor to help his or her downline as much as possible. By helping the people you sponsor become leaders, you help yourself. In the corporate world, you have to get pulled up from the top, but in network marketing you get pushed up from below. The more successful your downline becomes, the more successful you become; all ships rise with the tide, so to speak. This "Win-Win" nature of network marketing is quite the turnabout from the corporate structure. As you can imagine, it's also a major attraction for corporate employees seeking the fullness of their earning potential.

SECURITY

In the corporate world, you have no guarantees that your job will be there when you wake up tomorrow. As an "at will" employee, your company can essentially fire you at their will. If your job is a union position you have a bit more protection but you are still subject to layoffs. How many people do you know who have given their entire professional lives—in some cases two or more decades—to a company, only to be let go suddenly?

As a network marketer, you are an *independent business owner.* You are not an employee subject to termination at any time for any reason. You are in business for yourself.

COMPETITION

Many will argue that competition in the workplace produces excellence; it requires you to improve your skills if you want to advance. While this is true, competition also breeds contempt, betrayal and dejection. Competition can cause you to lose a grip on your ethics and morals, to do things that you wouldn't normally do. For you to climb the corporate ladder, you have to replace the person on the rung above you. For every person who gets the promotion, there are several who do not. There may be a thin veil of trust and teamwork, but all too often there is suspicion and scheming just below the surface. Everyone watches their back.

As we previously mentioned, there is a cooperative "Win-Win" dynamic at work in network marketing. Throughout your organization—all the way up and all the way down—the best results are produced only when everyone works as a team.

OPPORTUNITY

In the corporate workplace, you are subject to age, race, gender, social and other kinds of discrimination. Though such discrimination is illegal, it exists nonetheless. Discrimination can play a role in whether or not you are hired or promoted, how much you will earn and whether or not you keep your job.

The network marketing opportunity, however, is open to anyone. Success is not based on your age, the color of your skin, your orientation or whether or not you come from a prominent family. Network marketing is not an exclusive opportunity, but an *inclusive* one. Everyone has the chance to attain a lifestyle that is far better than most people have.

LEVERAGE

As long as you work a job, you will trade your time for money. The amount of your check next payday is directly tied to the amount of time you put into the job. Work more, earn more. Work less, earn less. This is an inescapable limitation of working for someone else.

Compare that to network marketing, where you have the opportunity to build a business that does not require you to "report to work" every day. You do this by teaching and mentoring others to build their own businesses.

Let's say that you have seven people that you have enrolled (see Fig. 2.3.). Let's also say that each of you puts five (5) hours per week into your own businesses. Including your five (5) hours that is 40 hours of effort each and every week. The beauty of the network marketing system is that you only directly produce five (5) hours of work, but you are paid for the full 40 hours!

This is known as "leveraging" your time and it is how you can build a full-time income on a part-time basis. You invest your time in helping others and that investment results in future income for you with limited time commitment. Think about the implication of this as it duplicates throughout your business. Instead of you and seven others in your business, what if there are seven *hundred* others? How about seven *thousand?* That's 35,000 hours of effort per week being conducted in your business, week after week, month after month, year after year. And your part is only five hours. Isn't that amazing?

U.S. industrialist J. Paul Getty, at one time the richest living American, often said, "I would rather make 1 percent on the efforts of 100 people than 100 percent on my own efforts." Now, you understand why!

Fig. 2.3

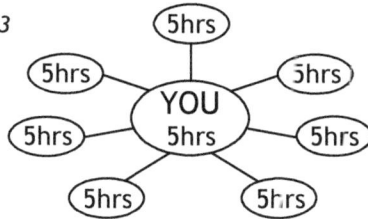

SCALABILITY

In the corporate world, there are expectations regarding the amount of time and effort you put into the job, as well as a minimum level of productivity. Your supervisor is responsible for making sure you get the job done right and in the allotted amount of time. If you don't, you may be reprimanded, disciplined or even fired.

In network marketing, no one is going to terminate you because you aren't working hard enough. If you are not productive, the company is not going to call and put pressure on you to work harder. You work as hard as you wish. It is after all *your* business. Moreover, you are given time to grow into your business, to learn the necessary skills and to grow personally as you tackle challenges you have not before faced.

RESIDUAL INCOME

Arguably, the most striking difference between network marketing and the corporate workplace is residual income. The day you stop working a job is the day they stop paying you. If you own a small business, you can sell it and perhaps make a tidy sum but your days of making a profit are over. As a network marketer, however, you have the opportunity to earn residual income. Residual income pays you long after you've stopped working and if you have built a strong enough foundation, will pay you for the rest of your life with little effort on your part.

Residual income is produced by doing something once and being paid for it over and over and over again. A prime example of residual income (also referred to as "royalty" income) is the recording industry. If you were to perform a hit song, you would only need to write, produce and record it once. Each time a copy of that song was sold, you would receive a payment in the form of a royalty. Elvis Presley died in 1977, yet 35 years later his estate earns some $60 million annually, much of it residual income from sales of his records.[10]

In network marketing, you build residual income primarily in two ways. The first is through a customer base. You acquire a customer, which is a one-time effort. This effort may last several months as you help the customer adapt the product to his or her daily routine, but it is a one-time effort nonetheless. At some point, the customer is encouraged to order on his or her own. Some may even choose to sign up for automatic monthly orders, also called "autoship." This income is residual because you are not required to be part of the process. It happens without you.

The second way to build residual income is through teaching and mentoring others in the business. You train them to become leaders and this effort pays you residual income long after your coaching and mentoring sessions end. This form of residual income is ultimately the most lucrative and also more secure. It is the most lucrative because instead of building your business one customer at a time, you build other business centers (people you enroll or sponsor) that each bring in lots of their own customers. It tends to be more secure because you have people below you who have invested their hopes and their future in this business. Their commitment level is many times greater than that of a customer who is simply using a product.

When Charlie Emmenecker, of Sylvania, Ohio was introduced to network marketing, he saw very quickly how this business model far surpassed what his golf business could offer him:

> I had always dreamed of earning a six-figure income and having the freedom to enjoy it. For years I thought the golf profession would afford me that opportunity, but big business began to change how the industry was run. I didn't like what I saw.

Nonetheless, I still had the Dream. And. I like to help people. I really enjoy getting a "thank you" or a hug. In golf, it wasn't unusual to get a phone call from someone who would exclaim that they broke 80 for the first time and were having the time of their life. It was great to hear that.

The difference between network marketing and the golf business is that I got paid to build the golf clubs once. I got paid to give the golf lesson once and that was it. I saw that I needed a business that was going to continually pay me on a residual basis. I didn't have the several hundred thousand dollars to buy a McDonald's or another franchise, and I also knew what that type of business meant in terms of a 20-year or so commitment.

Then, in 2003 I was introduced to a network marketing opportunity through a friend. He handed me a cassette and said, "Listen to this. It may be the most important thing you do the rest of your life." And, indeed it has turned out to be exactly that.

I worked at it very part-time at first, about 12-16 hours per week. But, in less than eight months I saw that I was going to replace the income from my golf business and my golf school. In one year I was able to close the golf school and go into this business full-time. But, that was still no more than 35-40 hours a week. I now have the income *and* the freedom I had always dreamed about.

Snowball Effect

Do you remember making a snowman as a kid? (Those of you grew up in warmer climates will have to use your imagination.) You started by packing some snow together in your hand, then packed more on top of it and eventually put it on the ground and rolled it. As you continued to do that, more snow packed onto the ball making it bigger and bigger.

Your network marketing business is similar. You start with a handful of activity, but through hard work and persistence you are soon "rolling." The more you roll the snowball, the larger it gets. Imagine now, that instead of making a snowman you are attempting to make a huge snowball, larger than any you have ever seen. Imagine also that you are pushing that snowball uphill. It's not easy, is it? The same will happen in your business, as there will be days when it is really hard to push because you are tired and frustrated. It happens with every business on the face of the earth.

But, you also know that if you can get the ball to the top of the hill, it will roll down the other side on its own. So, you keep your eye on that goal and keep pushing even when it's hard and even when you want to stop. Along comes your upline to encourage you and help you push the snowball.

And, then one day it happens: you reach the top and the snowball starts to lean over the edge of the other side of the hill. It slips away from you and starts rolling downhill. As it does, it picks up momentum and more snow. It just gets larger and larger on its own. At this point, you couldn't stop it if you tried!

Imagine your business doing the very same thing. Imagine your downline duplicating your efforts over and over and over again. Imagine waking up in the morning to learn that your business grew overnight in another part of the world while you were sleeping!

It's all about duplication; that's the key. Duplication is teaching, modeling, encouraging and mentoring. Through duplication, you build residual income, which can lead to complete financial and time freedom.

Quick Review: How Network Marketing Works

1) Network marketing continues to grow in popularity worldwide. In a recent 10-year period, the global sales force nearly doubled.

2) Network marketers are independent business owners who report only to themselves. They have a team of advisors and mentors (called an "upline") and a team of people that they are responsible for advising and mentoring (called a "downline").

3) Both employees and traditional business owners find many benefits in network marketing that are not available through their current job or business, such as low start-up costs, little to no ongoing costs and the ability to scale their business to fit their personal life.

4) The network marketing business model provides for residual income, which is the key to true financial and time freedom.

Exercise

1) Describe any frustrations or limitations you have in your current job or business. (If you are full-time in network marketing, describe those you *used* to have.)

2) Explain how you think a network marketing business can help you overcome those frustrations and limitations.

THREE

Stream of Contacts

If you purchased this book because you are looking for a step-by-step guide to network marketing, the next several chapters is where you will find it. If you follow these steps and become good at them, you can build a solid business.

If you want to build a business that gives you true freedom, however, becoming good at these steps will not be enough. You will need to be good at them and do them *hundreds of times over.* In other words, you will have to talk to a massive amount of people.

That said, let's get to it straight away. The process of building a solid and dynamic network marketing business has four basic parts:
1) Stream of Contacts
2) The Invitation
3) The Presentation
4) Follow-Up

We'll discuss each of these in successive chapters, beginning with your Stream of Contacts.

Capitalizing Your Business

In the business world, there is a term called "start-up capital." Start-up capital is the money you invest to start your business. This may be money you already have, but for most people it is money they have to borrow. If you were to start your water gun company, you would use this money to lease or buy a building, purchase equipment and vehicles, buy inventory and pay licenses and government fees.

In network marketing, you do not need the building, the equipment and the large inventory. But, you still need start-up capital. In this case, your capital is *relationship* capital, your stream of contacts. You have years—decades, even—of relationship capital invested in your family, friends, fellow employees and others. You have even more relationships through the clubs, civic groups, professional and trade associations, churches and other organizations to which you belong.

Studies show that each of us has an average of 750 people in our personal network.[1] That's 750 people we know well, people we used to know well and people we see or talk to occasionally. What this tells us is that we all have the ability to share our opportunity with literally *hundreds of people we already know.*

The value of these relationships, in terms of potential growth for your business, is immeasurable. Think about it for a moment. You are a good person, you're honest and trustworthy, you work hard, are respectful of other people, have a genuine interest in helping others and are fun to be around. Because of that, people value their relationship with you. What is any one of those relationships worth to your business? You cannot know for sure in the beginning, but each of them can mean tens of thousands of dollars (or more) for your business!

The value of relationship capital is often overlooked because our traditional view of investments and capital is focused on money, not people. A realty company can easily measure the amount of money invested in its building, office computers and licenses. But, the relationship capital that its agents possess—their personal stream of contacts that are potential buyers and sellers of real estate—can hardly be measured. Yet it is priceless, much more valuable than any amount of money invested in the company.

Building Equity

There is another term called "business equity." Business equity is a company's assets minus its liabilities (or debts) and is stated as a monetary value. The manufacturing machinery, fleet vehicles, inventory, office equipment and furniture are your business equity, tangible assets that have a value. Your customer base and other business relationships, often called "a book of business," also have a monetary value and are factored into your equity.

In your network marketing business, your network of people is your equity. The people you enroll and help and the people *they* enroll and help, and so on, form a strong downline that provides the financial freedom and security you desire.

Likewise, your upline has equity in you. The investment they make in you—the knowledge, wisdom and mentoring they provide—has a value. It is *their* equity.

The double blessing is that you will make many new friends, people you would have never met if not for your business. Some of these people will become your most trusted friends and confidants.

Remember that the value of your business is in your list of contacts and the people who make up your organization. It always comes back to relationships, human capital. When you understand and embrace this concept of valuing people above all else, you will have the correct mindset for building a profitable and stable business.

Knowing Your Market

To build a business, you will need to gather customers and sponsor business leaders. The people you identify to talk to are "prospective customers" or "prospective business partners," "prospects" for short. The process of engaging them is called "prospecting." As you prospect, you will find that people fit into one of three categories: your "hot" market, your "warm" market and your "cold" market. Each of these is distinct and understanding how they differ will help you develop a strategy for approaching people in each group.

Here is a definition of each:

1) *Hot market:* These are people you know well.
2) *Warm market:* These are a) people you know casually; and b) people you don't know but your hot market knows well.
3) *Cold market:* These are people you do not know and neither does your hot market.

Your hot market is closest to you and is the smallest of the groups. Your warm market is bigger and a bit further out from you, and your cold market is huge and farthest away. (See Fig. 3.1.)

Fig. 3.1

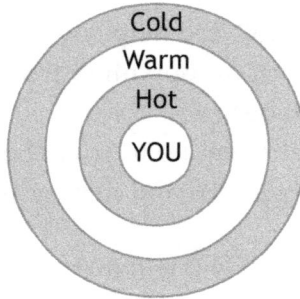

HOT MARKET

When you are excited about something, whom do you tell first? Think about your first date, when you got your first car, your first house, when your son scored the winning touchdown, or even when you found a great sale at the clothing store. You just had to tell someone, didn't you? It was probably your parents, siblings or a best friend that you called, right? When something wonderful happens in our lives, we naturally want to share it first with those we love and care about the most. This most certainly applies to your business opportunity!

Another reason we go to our hot market first is that we have a pre-existing and significant relationship with this group of people. They care about our happiness, success and well-being. They will be the most supportive and therefore the most receptive to hearing about our opportunity, whether or not they believe it is for them. (But, beware of the concerned family member who believes it is their responsibility to "save you" from network marketing!) This group will also be the most forgiving when you make a blunder or if your presentation isn't polished.

This is the group that will be the most likely to make an appointment with you, come to your in-home presentation or attend one of your company's opportunity meetings simply because you asked. Because they know you, they won't require as much information before committing to the appointment. They will meet with you just for the sake of your company. It is always a good idea to let them know in advance that you have something specific to talk about—not necessarily *what* that something is, just that you have a specific reason for meeting.

This prevents them from being surprised if they were thinking this was just a social meeting.

Many people in your hot market will purchase your products not because they need them or want them, but because they want to support you. No matter their motive for buying, don't worry. They are doing so because they care about you. Many of them will continue to purchase the products because they will discover that they like them. Some will become a great source of referrals and some will grab hold of the opportunity. Your business will be off to a strong start!

WARM MARKET

Your credibility in the warm market is not as strong as in your hot market, but you have at least *some* influence—a foot in the door, so to speak. The young lady you buy your morning coffee from, the woman behind the counter where you drop off your dry cleaning, the man who delivers the stuff you order on the Internet, the people who work for other companies in your building—you see these folks often and even if you don't know their name, *some* relationship already exists. Developing that relationship to a point where you can introduce your opportunity should be quite natural.

Your warm market also consists of people that you do not know, but are acquaintances of your hot market. This is your co-worker's neighbor, your uncle's chiropractor and your insurance agent's son who lives two states away. You have no relationship with these people whatsoever, but because your hot market knows them you have some built-in credibility. Always ask for referrals from your hot market. If you don't, you are missing great opportunities to build your business.

COLD MARKET

Your cold market is all of the people that neither you nor your hot market has ever met. Whereas this is by far the largest market—think of the billions of people on the earth—it is also the hardest and typically most frustrating. For these reasons, we recommend that you not venture into the cold market until you have exhausted your other two. This is the place where you will likely spend a considerable amount of money on advertising and other methods to acquire leads. The cold market can be profitable, but it can also be expensive and disheartening. You will soon learn that people who don't know you often believe they have a license to be rude and obnoxious. (Although, we can also say the same of certain family members, can't we?!)

A much higher percentage of your contacts in the cold market will be dead ends. Expect a high rate of "No's." Don't expose yourself to the cold market before you are financially able and mature enough to handle it. If you do venture into the cold market, be sure to wear your thick skin. It's called "cold" for a reason!

Family And Friends

Right now, many of you reading this book have a pit in your stomach. The thought of calling your hot market to tell them about your business opportunity makes you queasy. You are desperately hoping for a way to build this business without having to go to your friends and family. *Anything but that!*

Well, we are not going to tell you that you *must* talk to your family and friends. After all, this is *your* business and ultimately it is you who makes the decisions. But, take it from Ginny Fiscella: you don't know what—or rather *whom*—you might be missing:

> We had moved from Phoenix to Kansas City so we could raise our children close to their grandparents. Our girls were 2½ years old and two months old at that point. Moving meant I had to quit my job, but that was okay because I had wanted to be a stay-at-home mom anyway. But, four months into this routine day after day and night after night, seven days a week, I felt a loss of my identity. I didn't want to put my children in daycare because that would defeat the purpose of me being home. But, I knew I had to find big people time.
>
> I had never heard of direct sales before. One night at a family dinner, my sister gave me a catalog for a jewelry company. She said, "Ginny, my friend had a jewelry party. I thought you might like to place an order to help her out." When I got to the back page of the catalog it said, "Do you want to be a representative?" I was intrigued. I thought this might be a way to get out a couple nights a week, have my big people time and make some money.

So, I signed up and started booking some parties but I wasn't really telling many people. That changed when my best friend recruited herself to my business. She yelled at me. She said, "How selfish of you to keep this to yourself! I want to be a rep." You see, I was so careful about not being pushy to my friends and family; but, I realized that I never even informed them. After my best friend yelled at me and recruited herself, she was able to put all three of her sons in sports at once because of this business. She said, "How many other people did you miss in a year, Ginny?" And I said, "A lot." That's when the light bulb went on.

I went back to those people. I went back to each person that was either a hostess or customer of mine and I called them and said, "I believe I owe you an apology. I never offered you my business. I want you to know that it's an opportunity." The response I got was flooring. It just broke my heart. Some of the women said to me, "I thought I wasn't good enough and that's why you never asked." Others said, "I didn't know I could. I thought this was just your own personal jewelry company." It was devastating to me that I had never shared the opportunity with them.

I said, "From here on out, everyone who is within a three-foot radius of me gets to know what I do. What they choose to do with the information is up to them. I am never going back to feeling guilty again."

That's when my business really took off and started growing. When I started this business, I would have told you that I just wanted to find myself. But, it turned into more than that.

Much more, indeed. Twelve years after starting her business, Ginny reached Sterling Director, the highest level of her company's pay plan. She is the first in history to get there and unsurprisingly, is the highest paid among some 40,000 representatives. Moreover, Ginny has helped create more six-figure earners than anyone else in her company.

If you are still hesitant to talk to your family and friends, that is certainly your prerogative. Just understand that you might be doing your business a great disservice. Moreover, think about the disservice you might be doing to other people. Do you want to have the same regrets Ginny had?

Not contacting the people you already know means you have to talk to strangers. That typically makes the business more difficult. First, you subject yourself to a much higher rate of "No, not interested." Are you prepared for that? Second, building new relationships takes time, meaning you have to put many additional hours into your business. Are you prepared for *that*? Third, if you choose to advertise (and do it effectively), you have to spend a lot of money. A LOT! Are you prepared for *THAT*?

This industry is chock-full of people who weren't looking for a business, but thanks to their sister, dad, son, aunt, nephew, best friend or neighbor, have a life they never imagined. If someone in your life loses their home (or worse, their marriage) because they couldn't make enough money to support their family and you had a possible solution but didn't tell them about it, can you live with that? If your next door neighbor or (for heaven's sake) your brother shows up at an open meeting as someone else's guest, can you live with *that*?

We understand your hesitancy to approach friends and family. It's natural, particularly for people who are new to the business. But, it's also the result of fear-based thinking. It's the result of not believing enough in what you're doing. It's based on the self-defeating notion that anyone we approach is doing us a favor just for listening.

To be successful in this business, you need to arrive at a place where you believe you are doing *them* a favor, that what you have is a gift.

Make Your List

So, your first job is to make your list of contacts, to put your relationship capital to work! Go to your local office supply store and purchase a small blank notebook that has at least 100 pages. Buy one that is small enough that it is easy to carry with you in your handbag, briefcase or backpack. You will want to have this with you at all times. Begin writing down names of people you know. Don't filter, but instead write down every person whose name comes to mind.

If you are highly computer efficient, you may want to use a database or spreadsheet to organize your list. This is okay, just as long as you can take that electronic document with you on your laptop computer or other device. Throughout the day there will be several instances where something jogs your memory and you think of another person to add to your list, so have it with you at all times. Write that person's name down immediately; don't count on your ability to remember it later.

Don't put off making your list. It needs to be done right away! In fact, you don't even need to have started your business before making your list. If you are still considering what company you want to join, having your list ready to go will give you a fast start once you decide. When you have at least 100 names on your list, go over the list personally with your sponsor or other upline member. Put a star next to the 20 people you want to talk to first. Tell your sponsor how you know that person and what made you star them. Your upline will help you develop a thought process for calling each of those 20 people. Going over the list with another person is an important exercise for these reasons:

1) It makes you write the list down;
2) It makes you prioritize the list; and
3) It makes you think about why those top 20 people are important to you.

The reason you start with the 20 people you "starred" is because these are typically people you know best, people you are comfortable talking to and who tend to be supportive of you.

CHICKENS & TURKEYS

You will be tempted to exclude people from your list because you think they are already successful and wouldn't have an interest in your opportunity. You know that they have the big income, the nice house, the luxuries, the lifestyle. But, here is what you *don't* know about them: they may have what *you* want but not what *they* want.

Some of them have money but no time. Some of them have money and time, but are unchallenged. (Successful people need challenge in their lives; they thrive on it.) Some of them have time and money and are challenged, but they don't feel a connection to what they are doing; it's just a paycheck. These are the people who are ripe for your opportunity. Don't make an assumption that could be very costly to your business. Put them on your list!

There will also be some that you are afraid to call, which probably includes most of the aforementioned people. For some reason or another, you really fear calling these people. Perhaps their current success in business intimidates you. Maybe it's their personality. You may run in the same professional or social circles and in your mind they hold a place above you. These people make up what is called your "chicken list"—at this moment you are too chicken to call them!

Write their names down nonetheless so that when you have the courage to call you won't have forgotten them. Most people who have built huge network marketing businesses will tell you that one of their key leaders was someone on their chicken list. Put successful people on your list, especially if they are people you are afraid to call!

In addition to a chicken list, you will have a "turkey list." These are people you don't respect, who are self-centered, negative or undisciplined. Don't spend one minute with these people. If you were to sponsor them, their bad habits and attitude would only frustrate you and spread like a cancer throughout your organization. Remember, you are the owner of your business and you have a right to determine who your business partners are. Don't spend time with turkeys; they don't deserve what you have!

Quick Review: Stream Of Contacts

1) Start with your hot and warm markets.
2) The cold market is only for the thick-skinned.
3) Don't delay making your list; do it right now!
4) Carry your list with you everywhere you go. You never know when you will think of people to add to it.
5) Don't filter. Add everyone you think of, including people you are afraid to approach.
6) Review your list with your sponsor or other upline. Tell them about the people you care about most.

People You Already Talk To

Parents	Financial advisor	Dry cleaner
Grandparents	Doctor	Video store staff
Siblings	Chiropractor	Telemarketer
Children	Dentist	Hotel reservationist
Cousins	Optometrist	Travel agent
Aunts / Uncles	Masseur / Masseuse	Bank teller
Friends	Accountant	Barber / Hair stylist
Neighbors	Attorney	Roofer
Former neighbors	Florist	Plumber
Co-workers	Veterinarian	Furnace / AC
Former co-workers	Pet groomer	Lawn service
High school classmates	Tailor	Landscaper
College classmates	Baker	Tree trimmer
Childhood friends	Butcher	Fellow parishioner
Former teachers	Landlord / Prop. Mgr.	Pastor / Minister
Your kids'...	Cleaning service	Professional Assoc.
Teachers	Painter	Trade Association
Daycare provider	Decorator	Fellow volunteers
Coach	Family photographer	Person who...
Music teacher	Carryout/Market staff	sold you something
Dance instructor	Car wash owner	worked on your car
Classmates' parents	Restaurant owner	fixed your computer
Bus driver	Waiter / Waitress	works at the gym
Scout leader	FedEx/UPS driver	takes your payment
Insurance agent	Postal carrier	gave you a business
Realtor	Pizza driver	card

FOUR

The Invitation

Once you have a list of names, you should start contacting your top 20 as soon as you can. The best possible start for your business is for you to have appointments within 48 hours of enrolling with your company. In order to set those appointments, you are going to have to make some phone calls. This is what we call the Invitation or Inviting step, where you invite your prospect to look at your opportunity.

Get Organized

Prior to calling someone on your list, write their name down on a new page in your notebook, along with their phone number(s) and the date you are calling them. Make notes about your conversation, including anything they said that was significant (for instance, their anniversary is this week, their kids are sick, the kids are going on a school trip, they had an argument with the boss today, etc.). We can't always remember the names of our friends' spouses, kids and significant others so be sure to write down names, as well as ages of kids and grandkids.

Do this for every contact you call. If you get their voicemail, make a note of the time you called and that you left a message. Don't put more than 2 or 3 names per page so that you have plenty of space for notes about your conversations.

What Do I Say?

Far and away, the No. 1 question new network marketers have is "What do I say to people?" That's not surprising, given that most new network marketers know nothing about sales and, if they're out talking to people right way don't know enough about their business to speak confidently.

An even bigger factor, generally, is fear. Most of us are not comfortable in sales positions, either because we lack self-confidence or have the impression that we have to bother people and convince them to do something they don't want to do.

The best advice we can give you is to be excited and speak from your heart. This is where it becomes critical that you believe in what you are doing. When engaging people, your excitement and passion are much more important than your knowledge. Be excited; and, keep it real. If you sound like you should be on a game show—*Congratulations, you've just won the opportunity to start your own business!*—you'll lose your prospect. People can spot fake enthusiasm a mile away.

Use "You" Messages

When approaching prospects, it is natural to say something like "I'd like to show you what I'm doing" or "I'd love for you to look at this." Sounds reasonable, right? But, think about what you are really saying. You are telling them what *you* would like. *I'd like to show you this.* The truth of the matter is that prospecting isn't about what *you* want.

Everybody already has plenty of other people wanting something from them; your prospects don't need more of the same from you. One of the biggest misrepresentations of network marketing is that we just want something from the people we prospect. Well, saying "I'd like to" or "I'd love to" doesn't help dispel that notion.

You should use as many "you" messages as possible. For example, "You really need to take a look at this" or "You need to know what this is doing for people." Do you see the difference? Using "you" messages makes the conversation about the prospect, not you. It gives you a much better posture when you take the focus off of what you would like to accomplish and put it on how the prospect might benefit from your opportunity. Using "you" instead of "I" may seem trivial, but it can make a huge difference in how the prospect processes what you say.

Working Your Hot Market

Remember that people in your hot market are the most likely to be receptive to your invitation and therefore you have more freedom to be direct with them. Your conversation may go like this:

You: *Barb, this is Mary. I found something that you need to hear about. When are you available?*

   Barb: *What is it? Is it those pumps you've been looking for?!*

You: *No (laughing), it's not that! It's a way for me—and maybe you—to take control of our future. What's good for you?*

   Barb: *Uhm, how about lunch tomorrow? Let's say 11:30 at our usual spot.*

You: *Sounds good. See you then.*

If Barb is not agreeable, you might try a slightly different approach:

You: *Barb, this is Mary. I found something that you need to hear about. When are you available?*

   Barb: *What is it, Mary? Is this one of those business things, because if it is I can tell you right now it's not for me.*

You: *Barb, we know each other well so I think I'm on solid ground in saying this: you need to hear about this. You need to check it out. Is it for you? Who knows? What I do know is that the people I care about need to hear about it. Are you free tomorrow for lunch?*

   Barb: *Oh, well, since you put it that way, okay. Let's say 11:30 at our usual spot.*

You: *Sounds good. See you then.*

Did you notice that there were several "you" messages in that conversation? There is strength and posture in those examples. Now, notice how using "I" messages makes the invitation easy to reject:

You: *Hey, Jim, how are you doing? I'm calling because I'd like to show you what I'm doing now. I found a way to make extra money and I am so excited about it. I am really going to go places with this. I'd really love to have you join me, too. I'd like to meet with you real soon.*

   Jim: *(gulp) Uh…uhm…I'm really busy right now.*

RECONNECTING WITH OLD FRIENDS

We all have people that we've lost touch with, right? Well, it's not really appropriate to call someone after 10 years and right away launch into your opportunity, is it? So, what do you do? Many network marketers would suggest you do some catching up and then find a clever way to steer the conversation toward your real purpose, which is to talk about your opportunity. Be careful in doing this, though. When you disguise the real reason you are calling, you run the risk of the person on the other end of the phone feeling they've been manipulated.

You may already know what we're talking about because you've experienced it. You are having a great "how-have-you-been?!" conversation, laughing and talking about each other's kids and how much they've grown...and then it happens. You mention your opportunity and it's like you just dropped a bomb. The whole tone of the conversation changes; you can hear it in their voice. They feel like you set them up. Can you blame them?

Instead, be upfront from the beginning. Try something like this:

You: *Hey, Jack, it's Bill Smith, your former neighbor. It's been a long time, hasn't it?*

Jack: *Yeah, it has. Nice to hear from you, Bill. How have you and Susan been?*

You: *We're doing great, thanks for asking. Jack, I know we haven't talked in a long time and we've kind of lost touch. And, I really want to reconnect with you and catch up on things. But, I have to tell you that the reason I am calling today—I know this is out of the blue—is because I have found something that you and Jill really need to hear about...*

Working Your Warm Market

When talking to people in your warm market, your strategy will need to be a little different. Let's say you are calling a prospect referred to you by a friend, someone in your hot market. When asking people in your hot market for referrals, be sure to ask why they thought of that person. Try to learn a little about how they know that person, as well.

You still want to use "you" messages, but you also need to use your friend's connection to the prospect. Remember that any time you call someone, it is good manners to ask if you have reached them at a good time; in the case of a warm market prospect it is essential. It is helpful, too, if you compliment the person you are calling (just be sure to do it genuinely). Hopefully, your friend has told you enough about the prospect for you to be able to do this. You may also want to make a comment about how you know the person who gave you their name.

You: *Hello, Lisa?*

Lisa: *Yes, speaking.*

You: *Lisa, my name is Bill Smith. I'm a friend of Jack Jones. He gave me your name and number. Am I reaching you at a good time? Do you have a minute or two?*

Lisa: *Yes, I have a little time. How can I help you?*

You: *Jack tells me that you work for the same company. Are you a surveyor, too?*

Lisa: *Yes, we've been working together for about five years now.*

You: *I see. I've known Jack quite a while, too. We were neighbors for about 10 years. Great guy!*

Lisa: *Yes, he is.*

You: *Well, Lisa, the reason for my call is that we're expanding our business in this area and we are looking for people who may want to be a part of that. I asked Jack who he knows who is sharp, responsible and an overall quality person. You were the first person he mentioned.*

Lisa: *That was nice of him!*

You: *Yes, he obviously thinks highly of you! Lisa, I cannot guarantee that we will be able to work together, but let's sit down and discuss it. What is your availability in the next two days?*

What about the person behind the counter at the dry cleaner? You might use an approach such as this the next time you stop by:

You: *Hi, how are you today, Claire?*

Claire: *I'm doing okay. How are you?*

You: *I am doing very well! Thank you for asking.*

Claire: *Dropping off some items today?*

You: *Yes, here they are...Claire, I realize we don't know each other well. We see each other maybe once a month at best, right? Well, what if I told you that there is a way for people like you and me to earn extra income, that we could do it at our own pace and that we would have great teachers. Would that be of interest to you?*

SCRIPTS

Be careful about scripts, where you write out word-for-word what you are going to say. Scripts are tempting because they can give us more confidence when we're nervous or inexperienced. But, unless you are a pro at using scripts, you will sound like you are reading—or worse, like a robot:

Hello…Jim?…This…is…Sally…calling…How…are…you……to-day?

The person on the other end will smell it out pretty quickly, the conversation will be awkward and your credibility will take a quick nose dive.

You may want to jot down some thoughts or bullet points to refer to while on the phone. This will help you stay on track and organize your thoughts. But, avoid reading something word for word. Share from your heart and leave the scripts to the actors!

FOCUS ON THE BUSINESS

Should you lead with the products or should you lead with the business? (In other words, what should you talk to your prospect about first?) That is a question that gets debated heavily in the industry. We believe that you should lead with the business. Will there be a few rare occasions when you want to lead with the product or service? Yes. For instance, if your company sells health products and your prospect has an apparent and serious health problem, you may want to say, "Bill, my company's products may be able to help you. You need to hear more about them." (Bear in mind that at some point you also need to let Bill know there is a business opportunity; many people with serious health issues have a great financial need as a result of their illness.)

If you make a habit of looking for customers, customers are all you'll find. You won't find business leaders. But, if you go looking for leaders, you will find customers by default and you will also find the leaders you are seeking. Let's suppose you are talking to a prospect about your business opportunity and she says, "No, thanks." You can still say, "Well, how about the products?" She may very well say, "Yes."

If, on the other hand, you talk first about the products and she says, "No, thanks," you are done. You can't come back and say, "Okay, I understand that you aren't interested in the products, but would you like to make money building a business around them?" That would be ridiculous, right?!

Practice!

We have given you just a few suggestions on how to do the Invitation in a way that is genuine and from the heart, yet strong in posture. For you to become comfortable with this step, you will need to practice. Find a partner and role-play. The more you do it in advance, the more confident and proficient you will be. Practice, practice, practice!

What Not to Say or Do

Not saying the wrong thing is just as important as saying the right thing. Here are some common mistakes that can impede your ability to build a business and tarnish the reputation of the network marketing industry. Work to avoid them.

Misleading Statements

Never lead your prospects to believe something that isn't true. For instance, don't say or imply that you are offering them a job. Don't hide the fact that you operate a business that sells goods or services. (That's what businesses do!)

Likewise, do not disguise the fact that what you do is network marketing. A lot of networkers struggle mightily with this. *Should I tell them it's network marketing? What if I do and then they're no longer interested?*

We are going to make this very easy for you: Tell them it's network marketing…if they ask. Always be honest and forthcoming. However, if they don't raise the issue, there is no reason for you to, either. If it matters to them that this is network marketing, they will ask you.

And, when the prospect *does* ask, don't assume it's because they dislike network marketing. They might love network marketing, or may just be curious. Not everyone who asks "Is this network marketing?" has a negative attitude toward the industry. Some people will be more interested because it *is* network marketing.

Engage your prospect in honest, open dialogue. When we mislead people we open the door to a host of problems. Perhaps a prospect will join despite your deception. But, a relationship birthed from trickery or intentional vagueness is doomed. In these instances, the prospect did not join because she or he is sold on the opportunity, but because of your manipulation. Ultimately, your new recruit will likely quit or at the very least be unproductive. Moreover, you have given them a license to tell everyone they know that you and your company are not truthful and forthcoming.

Some prospects may even join you *because* of your deception, particularly if they are someone who frequently practices it themselves. In this case, there is a high probability that similar deception will duplicate throughout the organization that prospect builds under you, and the problem becomes magnified.

By misleading people, you not only damage your own business but you undermine the integrity of an industry that deserves better.

Convincing

It's a common refrain among frustrated network marketers: "If I could only convince her that she needs this." Networkers who make laments like this fail to understand that it is not their job to convince people. Their job (and your job) is to present the opportunity or product, and then let the prospect decide. Often, that decision will be "No." And, when the answer is "No," you should go no further.

Remember: a man convinced against his will is of the same opinion still. Convincing people may get you some initial sales, but just as it is with misleading people your success will be short lived. People want to buy; they don't want to be sold. Let them make up their own minds.

"I don't have much time right now"

This is often used in the appointment-setting process as a way to discourage the prospect from asking questions. When you say "I don't have any time to talk right now," what do you suppose the prospect thinks? *You don't have time to talk right now? Aren't you the one who called ME? This sounds suspicious. He must want something from me.*

While it is true that you don't want to start answering questions when setting the appointment, you also don't want to give that person reason to refuse to meet with you or to cancel the appointment later. It may be true that you really don't have much time when you call them. But, find a better way to say it. For instance:

Chuck: *Is this one of those pyramid deals?*

You: *Chuck, that is a great question and I'm sure you will have a lot more. Why don't we discuss it when we meet? I'll answer all of your questions at once.*

"I'LL BUILD YOUR BUSINESS FOR YOU"

Although network marketers may use this approach out of a genuine desire to help the prospect, it is not in the prospect's best interest to say this (much less do it!). Telling someone you will build their business for them and that all they have to do is connect you to their contacts, is wrong. First, it promotes the unhealthy notion that people can get something without having to work for it and we all know that is not true of this business. Worse yet, it duplicates. You have given your prospect a reason to tell his friends and family that all they have to do is call you and you will build their business for *them*, as well.

As a result, you will have a high dropout rate because no one has a commitment to the business. No one has invested or paid any kind of price. And, how much do we value things we don't pay for? Not much. You may have some initial success, but you will be working your tail off trying to stay up with all of the activity only to see your business erode over time.

APOLOGIZING FOR NETWORK MARKETING

Don't apologize for network marketing; there is nothing to excuse or justify. You are in an honorable industry. Be proud of what you do! Avoid statements like, "Yeah, I know it's network marketing but I'm doing it any way" and "I never would have believed I'd be doing something like *this*!" What you are essentially telling the other person is that you are involved in something that you do not believe in. Why would you ask someone to join something that you believe requires an apology?

NAME DROPPING

Don't try to sell your opportunity based on who else has joined. Telling your prospect that the local pastor, judge, sheriff, bank president or other high-profile person is a member of your company diminishes what you have. It sends the message to your prospect that the opportunity does not have enough merit to stand on its own and needs help to look attractive and legitimate.

Your prospects may want to validate the opportunity by doing research and due diligence on your company—in fact they *should*—but you should not attempt to do it for them by name dropping. Instead, let the attractiveness of your opportunity speak for itself. Then, personally introduce your prospect to those high-profile people at a company opportunity meeting or on the phone. This will allow you to borrow the strength of that person and will be much more impressive to your prospect than you dropping a name.

ARGUING

Occasionally, you will encounter prospects (or their friends and family) who want to argue with you. The argument may be about the network marketing business model. It may be about an ingredient in your product or a feature of your service. It may be about something you said. Some people just need to argue.

Don't feed their need. Walk away. Even if you're right and they're wrong it does you no good to continue. Winning an argument will not build your business. Instead, spend that time and energy on someone who appreciates what you have.

"IT'S EASY / ANYONE CAN DO THIS"

One of the great injustices in our business is when someone tells a prospect that network marketing "is easy," only for that prospect to have a rude awakening once they join. This business is not easy and we should not be telling people that it is.

We also need to be careful about saying "anyone can do this." While it is true that anyone *can* do this business, we don't want to mislead people into thinking it will come naturally to them. Always be upfront about the fact that network marketing, like all legitimate and sustainable businesses, requires a lot of hard work and skill.

Never mislead or exaggerate; nothing ruins the truth like stretching it.

"THE PRODUCTS SELL THEMSELVES"

This is another no-no. Nothing sells itself. If products sold themselves, the company wouldn't need us. Claiming something will "sell itself" caters to people's fear of sales and makes the business appear to be easy. Is it true that many people will want your product or service once you show them the benefits of using it? Of course! But, you have to *show* them. Don't tell your prospects that "people will be knocking on your door for this" because it never works that way. You have to go out and find people; they don't find you.

Similarly, not everyone will want your product or service once they do hear about it. We guarantee that some people will say it's too expensive, doesn't taste good, smell good or look good, or they simply aren't interested. That's just how it works. Not everybody wants a McDonald's hamburger or a Starbucks coffee and not everybody wants *your* product. When we tell people that "everyone will want this" and they sign-up and find out it's not true, they will come to the conclusion that we are untruthful or that they must be doing something wrong.

"YOU'D BE GREAT AT THIS"

Telling someone they would be good at something is a nice compliment and if you have said this to your prospects, we're sure you meant it sincerely. However, just like you shouldn't assume certain people won't be good at network marketing neither should you assume that certain people *will*.

The truth is that none of us has any idea how good any particular person will be at this business until they do it. Whereas this is not high on the list of things to avoid saying, try to eliminate it. Keep the focus on how your opportunity can help them, not on how good they might be at it.

PROMISES

Likewise, don't promise or lead people to believe they will be making a certain amount of money by a certain date. You cannot keep that promise, because the money they make depends on their actions, not yours. And, how can you possibly promise what others will do? Instead, promise that you will provide the training and mentoring that is necessary for them to be successful. The rest is up to them.

THANKING THE PROSPECT

Don't thank your prospect. It's a natural and polite thing to do, but don't thank people for looking at your opportunity *or* when they join your business. You are doing *them* the favor. They should be thanking *you*! This is especially true with friends and family, who often feel an obligation to participate in what you are doing. Don't reinforce the obligatory nature of their "help" by thanking them.

At your meetings, don't stand up and thank people for coming. Instead, say "We're glad to see you," "Welcome," or "We're glad you're here," but don't thank them. You may think this is a small thing, but it's not. Thanking another person means we are obligated to them. Psychologically, it improperly elevates them to a higher position.

SUPERLATIVES

Many network marketers feel it necessary to tout their opportunity as the best: the *best* products, *best* compensation plan, *best* management, *best* marketing strategy, and so on. Often, these superlatives will be perpetuated by the company itself, and in many cases *are arguably true.*

However, they mean nothing to your prospect. Your prospect will almost never care that what you have is the best in the industry. What matters to them is that your products and services work and that they can make money selling them. It is highly unlikely that a prospect will join your company because you are No. 1 and just as improbable that they won't because you are not No. 1.

If your products exceed government regulations or industry standards, you certainly should explain why. If your compensation plan is better than the industry average, go ahead and mention that, too.

But, avoid saying that your company is the best there is; in most cases you can't prove it and your prospect doesn't care anyway.

CRITICIZING ANOTHER COMPANY

Never criticize another company or network marketer. Don't ever say that what you have is better than "XYZ" company's. You don't actually know that unless you have studied XYZ company's products, and if you *have* then you need to spend less time researching other businesses and more time building yours.

If a prospect is using a competitor's product or service, ask if they are satisfied with their results. If they are, wish them continued success and move on. If they are not satisfied, offer to show them yours. But don't ever say, "Oh, you need to use what I have; it's a lot better than what you're using now."

Likewise, if your prospect is considering another opportunity don't say, "Oh, don't go with *that* company. You'll never make any money with them. Come with us instead." Criticizing another networker or company says little about them, but a lot about you. Don't stoop to such tactics.

Okay, we've just given you quite a bit of information about the things you shouldn't say or do. Admittedly, we have given you much more detail on what you *shouldn't* say than what you *should*. If you have been doing some of these things in your business, don't dismay. Just correct them going forward. We hope that you receive this in the spirit in which it is given: as good instruction, not condemnation. Be encouraged!

Expanding Your Market

You should always be looking for ways to add new people to your list of contacts. One sure-fire way to do this is to become an expert listener. Train yourself to listen for opportunities. That person in the elevator this morning who was complaining about her job, the delivery driver who was complaining about his bad back, the co-worker who said she wants to help her daughter with college tuition but doesn't have the money—these are all opportunities for you.

Remember, we all like to talk about our problems. Your radar should always be up listening for people's needs:

- *I don't have money;*
- *I don't have any time;*
- *I don't like what I do;*
- *I don't feel well.*

When you have these opportunities, do your best to get the person's telephone number. If you simply give them your business card, they will almost never call you back. This is because at that moment you do not have sufficient credibility. You are someone they just met who is kind and offered to help, but you are a stranger. If you are able to get their name and phone number, transfer this information to your list as soon as possible. Be sure to write down the date, the circumstances under which you met them and when you said you would be calling them.

You should also develop what is referred to as an "elevator speech." An élevator speech is a short description of your business, short enough that if someone on the elevator asks, "What do you do for a living?" you can answer before they step off at their floor. For example:

Prospect: *So, are you here on business?*

You: *Yes, I sure am.*

Prospect: *What do you do?*

You: *I help people make more money, make more free time or both, whatever they want.*

Prospect: *We could all use more of that.*

You: *That's for sure! If that's what you want, give me your number and a good time to call you.*

Here is a more intriguing approach:

Prospect: *What do you do?*

You: *I help people be free to do what they want when they want.*

Prospect: *How do you do that?*

You: *Give me your telephone number and a good time to call you; I'll explain it to you.*

Setting The Appointment

We've given you several ideas for inviting people to look at your opportunity. Here are some additional things to keep in mind when setting the appointment.

STOP TALKING

Once you have agreed on a time and place to meet your prospect, end the conversation or change the subject. Unseasoned network marketers often weaken a great invitation by continuing to talk after the prospect has committed. It is usually because the networker is excited about the upcoming appointment. *They actually said "Yes!"* Just remember that the purpose of the Invitation step is to set the appointment, not *do* the appointment.

ALWAYS CONFIRM

Always confirm your appointments. You will save valuable time and travel expenses by doing so. Many of your prospects will not show up for appointments either because they changed their mind and didn't bother to call you or they simply forgot. You should confirm your appointments twice: first, when setting the appointment and second, a few hours before the appointment. When you are setting the appointment, try to make sure your prospect understands that they are agreeing to meet you on a specific day at a specific time and place, much like if they were going for a job interview.

Here is how you might do this:

You: *Why don't we both get out our day planners right now and write our appointment in for Tuesday, Noon at Joe's Deli on Fourth and Main.*

Prospect: *Okay, got it.*

You: *Great. See you then…Oh, one more thing. You have my cell number. I know that things sometimes come up and if you have to reschedule, would you please call me as soon as possible?*

Prospect: *Sure.*

On the morning of the appointment:

> You: *Miguel, it's Larry. We have a lunch appointment today at Noon at Joe's Deli. I'm just calling to make sure we're still on.*
>
>> Miguel: *Yes, I'll be there.*
>
> You: *Great. See you then!*

Always confirm your appointments, expect that many people will reschedule or cancel and don't fret when they do. At least you won't have wasted your time waiting for a no-show. Instead, you will be using that valuable time for the next person.

TALK TO COUPLES TOGETHER

Try to schedule your appointments so that you are meeting with couples together. (This includes phone appointments.) Often, you will meet with a prospect who becomes quite excited only to have their spouse later quash that enthusiasm. This is what we call the "Spouse As Dream Stealer" syndrome (SADS). You won't be successful 100 percent of the time getting couples together, but strive to do so. Here is a way you might handle that situation:

> You: *Irene, you said that you are available this Wednesday at 7 p.m. and that works for me, too. Will your husband be available for this appointment as well?*
>
>> Irene: *No, they moved him to second shift at work so he won't be home until after midnight. Does he need to be there? I'll just tell him what it's about.*
>
> You: *Irene, it really would be better if we do this when your husband can be there, too. Here's why: you are going to be excited about what you see and you'll want to tell him all about it, but there will be too much to remember. It's better if he sees it for himself. Also, I have seen this happen too many times: one spouse comes to the appointment alone and they can't wait to get home to talk about it. When they do the spouse who wasn't there and can't appreciate what the other just saw says, "We're not going to do something like that." And, your Dream dies. Irene, believe me you don't want that to happen. If this is for you, it needs to be for both of you. If it's not for you, the two of you need to decide that together.*

Irene: *Oh, okay, I see what you mean. Let me see if he can meet Saturday and I'll call you back. Will Saturday work for you?*

You: *Yes, that will work. Can you let me know tomorrow? My calendar fills up pretty quickly so I'd like to be sure I'm available.*

Irene: *Yes, I can do that.*

You: *Wonderful! I'll talk to you tomorrow. Bye, now.*

PICK AN APPROPRIATE VENUE

Give some thought to where you will be meeting your prospect. If you will be having them talk to your upline via cell phone during the appointment, be sure to pick a relatively quiet place. This is especially true if you are having your upline talk to two prospects at once over the speaker on your cell phone. Beware of coffee shops; nothing is more frustrating than trying to speak over a whirring coffee grinder or mocha machine!

If you are meeting during the lunch hour, try to pick a place that is close to where the prospect works and that also has fast service. They will appreciate you doing that.

WHEN THEY START ASKING QUESTIONS

You will find out pretty quickly that most people start asking questions when you are attempting to set an appointment. You will also learn pretty quickly that he who asks the questions controls the conversation. That person can be you or it can be the prospect.

When the prospect starts asking questions, you will be tempted to start answering them. That's the natural and polite thing to do, right? Yes, but it's not the *right* thing to do. If you answer one question, the prospect will almost always ask another one. If you answer that one, they will ask another and so on until you have lost all control of the conversation.

When people start asking questions it is generally because they want to make a decision right there on the spot. We live in a fast-paced world and our day consists of making and managing hundreds of decisions. To cope, we have trained ourselves to analyze and decide quickly. Your prospects may be looking for just enough information to make an instantaneous decision so they can get on with their day. When we oblige them, we allow them to make a choice based on incomplete information and that choice is generally "No." What you have is too valuable to be considered lightly.

Other people will insist that you give them the name of the company because they want to do their own "research" before committing to an appointment. If you are talking to the prospect on the phone, you may even hear them typing your company's name into an Internet search engine as you speak! Whatever their reason, don't get into the habit of answering their questions during the Invitation step.

Never, ever lie to people or mislead them. These days, almost everyone has heard of network marketing. Most people are savvy and will figure it out long before you tell them, anyway. Here is how you might respond to questions:

Prospect: *Is this a sales thing? I mean, what's this about anyway? What would I have to do?*

You: *Great question. I'm sure you'll have more. Why don't we address that at the appointment?*

Prospect: *Why can't you just answer my question?*

You: *It's not that I don't want to answer your questions; I most certainly do. Let me ask you this: if I answer that question, will that be enough information for you to make a decision? I could answer all of your questions right now, but you would still have just a small picture of what this is all about. That's not enough for making an informed decision. Does that make sense?*

Prospect: *Okay, I suppose.*

You: *Great! I look forward to meeting with you.*

Did you notice in the above example how you answered each of your prospect's questions with a question? Is this because you are trying to be manipulative? No, it's because you don't want to lose control of the conversation. Your goal is to set the appointment. Your prospect will get his answers, but he should get them at the appropriate time. His decision should be an informed one.

Quick Review: The Invitation

1) Be excited and share from your heart. Be genuine!
2) Avoid saying "I" and instead use "you" messages.
3) Be careful with scripts. They can sound insincere.
4) Lead with your business opportunity, not the products.
5) Practice, Practice, Practice!
6) Never attempt to convince, never argue, mislead, criticize or promise.
7) Learn to be a good listener. People love to talk about their wants and needs.
8) Resist the urge to answer questions when you are setting the appointment.

Exercise

Imagine that you are about to pick up the phone and make some business calls to introduce people to your opportunity. Write out what you would say in each of the following instances. Use bullet points instead of writing out word for word. (Remember, we want to avoid using scripts.)

1) Calling a sibling or other close family member:

2) Contacting your best friend:

3) Catching up with an old friend you haven't talked to in a long time:

FIVE

The Presentation

You have successfully maneuvered through the Invitation step and you are now preparing for the Presentation. First, give some thought to what you are going to wear. You want to dress similarly to how you think the prospect will dress. For instance, if you are meeting with a farmer or mechanic after they get off work don't come dressed in a suit and tie. Likewise, if you are meeting with a white-collar professional or business owner, don't wear jeans. Use good judgment and you will avoid embarrassing moments.

Pay attention to your personal hygiene, including your breath. Don't be late. Leave earlier than you think is necessary to allow for heavy traffic and unexpected delays. If you are unfamiliar with the area, leave exceptionally early. If you are doing a phone appointment, call precisely at the scheduled time. Remember, you don't get a second chance to make a first impression!

It's All About The Other Person

The inexperienced networker typically comes to the appointment "locked and loaded." He has been a great student of his company's basic training and he can't wait to share with his prospect all of the great knowledge he has gained about the products, services, compensation and mission of the company. Before the prospect's backside has even hit the seat, the network marketer is pulling out presentation brochures, flip charts and samples of the products. He is excited!

With all of his materials in place, he proceeds to regurgitate all he has learned. An hour later, he finally takes a breath. Across from him sits a prospect who has long since tuned out.

Does that remind you of your first appointment? Have you blown people's hair back? If so, that's okay—we've done it, too! If you are brand new to network marketing, learn from those of us who have hosed people down: don't open the fire hydrant.

You have one goal at this appointment and that is to learn about the other person and what they need. Leave your sales tools in your bag; don't even get them out. Instead, have a conversation with the prospect about her needs, her wants, her Dream. How do you do this? *Ask her questions!*

In the previous chapter, we suggested that you make a record of your conversation when calling to set the appointment. Have those notes with you during the presentation and refer to them as necessary. Draw a horizontal line under the previous entry and below that line write the word "Presentation," the date and the location of your meeting. Here, you will record anything noteworthy your prospect says during the appointment. What are her passions? What is she most worried about? What business questions does she have?

You will have appointments where all you do is talk about the prospect's life. Just learning about her and asking questions will take up the entire time. You won't have the opportunity to go through your presentation. If that happens, don't worry; just set another appointment. For example, "Wow, look at the time! We didn't really get to the material, but that's okay. This was time well spent. It's important that I learn about you and what you are looking for. Why don't we set another time to get together?" You have just invested a significant amount of time in listening to your prospect; it is highly likely that she will agree to another appointment.

Some of us are naturally good at listening, some not so much. You may need to develop this skill. Practice it. Role-play with another person. Take it seriously. It will transform your business, but moreover it will deepen every relationship you have!

From Listening To Presenting

It is a good idea to rehearse your presentation. You will likely be nervous in the beginning and having the presentation down pat will make you more confident. The more presentations you do, the better you will become. No matter how much you rehearse, however, practice is not like the actual appointment. Don't think you have to be perfect; you don't! Just be enthusiastic and sincere. Your first few appointments will be poor to mediocre, your next few mediocre to good, the next couple good to above average and from there on you will be fantastic each and every time!

If you have done a good job of active listening and asking questions, you will have found a thread to use to introduce your story and your WHY. This is a great way to start your presentation. Here's how you do it:

Sherry, you were just sharing with me how you feel like your job is a dead end, that it no longer excites you. I heard you when you said you haven't had many raises in the last 10 years, and that the people entering your field right out of college are getting paid just as much as you are. That has to be disheartening.

You know, I had a lot of the same frustrations before I heard about this business.

From there, you tell your story. Be sure to share *your* hopes, *your* fears, and *your* Dream. Describe your life before you learned of this opportunity. Recall one of your worst days, how it made you feel, what went through your mind. Contrast that with the way you feel now and how the business has given you hope. You want to transfer that feeling from you to them.

You will not have personal experience with every situation you encounter. You may not have lost your job. You may not have a jerk for a boss. You may not be struggling to pay the bills. You may not have to send your children off to daycare. But, you will likely know someone in your business who *has* experienced those things. In these instances, use *their* story.

More than anything, be genuine. Share your heart. It's important that the prospect knows that you know what you want, and that you believe your business opportunity is going to help you get it.

The Products And The Company

Your presentation also should include ample information about your products and services and the company behind them. Explain how the products are unique, why they are effective and why they are competitive in the marketplace. Do you have a product that appeals to Baby Boomers? This generation is the largest consumer group in society and their buying power is immense. Perhaps your products are appealing to younger groups such as the X Generation or Y Generation. You need to be able to address the appeal of your products from a business perspective. After all, it is your products and services that drive your opportunity. Your prospect needs to believe that he or she can build a business around them.

Be sure to explain any achievements or notable experiences of the people in your line of sponsorship, as well as that of the company leadership. Stability and profitability are important, too. Your prospect needs to see that the company has a good track record and will be there for the long term.

Keep this part of the presentation relatively short; it should be no more than 10-15 minutes of a 60-minute appointment. As we mentioned before, the most important thing is to find out what your prospects want. The time for them to learn all of the details about your company and the products will come once they have joined.

Features Versus Benefits

A national hardware retailer held its annual company convention. The award for the top-producing store manager went to the same man for a fifth consecutive year. When asked to share how his store had outperformed every other store across the country—in the process breaking the company record for sales of drills—he gave a simple yet profound explanation:

"We just started asking our customers questions about their needs," he said. "We stopped selling drills and started selling holes."

That illustration should make it clear to you that it's the benefits of your product that are important, not the features. Your prospect will not care about the various features of your product as much as he does about how it will make him feel. He won't care about the inner workings of your compensation plan as much as he does about being able to make money. Are the features important? Yes. Are the details relevant? Certainly. These things validate your opportunity. However, more important to the prospect are what the products and the business can do for him. Don't become fixated on the features of the drill; show people the benefits of using it.

Bring The Compensation Plan To Life

When you present your compensation plan, try to explain how it works by using the prospect's vocation or profession as an example. Human beings learn only analogy; we take what we already know and use that knowledge as a basis to learn new things.

The concept of residual income can be difficult for people to grasp. So, when talking to a prospect, find out what they do for a living (or if they don't work find out what their favorite hobby is) and use what they already know to explain residual income. We'll give you an example. (You should write this out on paper using a diagram.)

You: *Tom, you said you are dispatcher for a trucking company, right?*

Tom: *That's right.*

You: *How many loads leave the plant every day?*

Tom: *About 50.*

You: *Well, Tom, wouldn't it be great if you could train someone to do what you do and for every truck that person dispatches—let's say he does the same amount as you, 50 per day—you would earn an extra $2?*

Tom: *Yes, I would love it!*

You: *Sure you would. That's $100 per day, right?*

Tom: *Right!*

You: *And, then let's say that the person you just trained trains three other people and because you trained the trainer, you get $1 for every truck those three dispatch, which would be how much more per day?*

Tom: *Another $150. That would be awesome!*

You: *Tom, those three each train three and that makes 9 dispatchers who are three levels away from you. Because you are also helping them just like you are helping the rest of the dispatchers, you earn 50 cents for each truck they dispatch, which would be how much?*

    Tom: *That would be 450 trucks multiplied by 50 cents, which is $225.*
You: *That's right. And, Tom, that is how generation royalties work. Royalty income is residual income, money you earn long after you stop working. In your case, you trained someone once and that effort continued to pay you over and over again. The more you invest in others, teaching and training them in this business, the more residual income you earn.*

    Tom: *I see that. Wow!*

Next, ask your prospect what a good initial income goal would be for their new business. Then, tailor the plan showing how he would earn that income.

    You: *Tom, you told me earlier that you would like to earn an extra $2,000 per month. If I recall correctly, you said that would replace your wife's income and she would be able to come home for good.*

    Tom: *That's right.*

You: *Okay, let's look at how you could do that.*

As you explain the compensation plan look for opportunities to say something like: *Tom, if you were to accomplish what I've explained thus far, you would be earning $500-$1,000 per month. Susan would be halfway home, wouldn't she?* You will also want to note when you hit his magic number:

    You: *Tom, tell me again how much per month we need to get to for Susan to come home.*

    Tom: *$2,000 per month.*

You: *Well, guess what? We're not even halfway through the compensation plan and look where your income is: it's $2,500 per month! Now, let's stop here for a second. Tell me what you are going to say to Susan when your business gets to this point. And, what do you think she'll say to you?*

Do you see the power in doing this? You are not just shoving numbers at your prospect. When you walk his Dream through your compensation plan, it comes alive!

Problem-Solution

Network marketing is a problem-solution business. You are looking for people who have a problem and who need (and want) your solution. You are looking for people who recognize that something is missing in their life: time freedom, financial security, a secure retirement, a greater sense of purpose to name a few.

Let's use Tom the truck dispatcher as an example. Suppose that as you asked Tom questions about his life, he revealed to you that his Dream would be to retire early and buy a house at the lake. He and Susan have always wanted to live on the water. Tom has a problem: he wants to retire early and have a better life but he does not currently have the ability to do so.

You have just shown Tom how your opportunity can bring Susan home and get him one step closer to his Dream. You have presented a solution. Now, you want to tie Tom's problem to your solution, you want to tie his Dream to your opportunity.

So, you ask him this question: *Tom, can you get what you want in life by doing what you are doing now?*

It's a simple question; the answer is either "Yes" or "No." You need to hear from Tom's mouth, in his own words the following: *No, I can't get what I want by doing what I'm doing right now.*

It is very important that Tom expresses this verbally. Our mind has an amazing ability to trick us into believing that if we don't talk about something it will go away or somehow get better. Tom needs to verbalize the fact that he can't get what he wants by continuing to do what he is currently doing. It needs to come to the surface.

Next, you have to emotionalize Tom's situation, disturb it. Note that we said you should disturb it, not *exploit* it. There is a difference and you must be careful not to manipulate people.

Tom, you just told me that unless something in your life changes, you will not get your Dream. How do you feel about that? If 10 years from now nothing has changed, can you live with that result?

At this point you have identified the need, you've had Tom verbalize it and you have addressed the emotion attached to it. Next, you need to paint a picture of the solution. The best way to do this is to use another story. Use the inspirational story of someone who was in a situation similar to Tom's and through your opportunity was able to realize his Dream. By doing this you will inspire Tom and give him hope, which can then move him to action.

Ask For A Decision

This is the point where new network marketers often struggle. They don't know how to ask for a decision. Out of fear, they wait for the prospect to self-commit. Well, guess what? The prospect will almost NEVER do this. They need you to guide them to a decision.

In sales, this is called "closing"—you are trying to close the deal. We don't particularly like the use of that term in this context. You aren't actually closing a deal, but instead *opening a door* to a new relationship. You are welcoming a new business partner. The important thing is that you want the prospect to make a decision about what he or she has just heard. You can do this in many forms. You might use one of the following or a combination:

You've shared a lot with me about... (the things in life you would like to have, how you'd like to feel better, how you would like to be out of debt). May I ask you a question: how badly do you want that?

Do you see how this business can help you get what you want and why people are so excited about this?

On a scale of 1 to 10, with 10 being the highest, how much does this appeal to you?

Conversely, don't oversell. After the prospect has made a decision—it doesn't matter if it is "Yes," "No" or "Let me think about it"—don't continue to sell and don't pressure them. Here are some examples:

Decision: *I'm ready to join. What do I do next?*
   Inappropriate response: *Great! You know, that new product we told you about is so incredible. You are going to just love it! And, when you start*

meeting the people that are behind this opportunity—oh, I can't wait to introduce you to them!

Appropriate response: *Wonderful! Welcome aboard! We can fill out the enrollment form right now if that works for you.*

Decision: *I'm afraid this isn't for me. No, thank you.*

Inappropriate response: *Are you sure? Like I said, we have a money-back guarantee so you're not really risking anything..*

Appropriate response: *Well, it was certainly a pleasure meeting you. We wish you all the best! Would it be okay for one of us to touch base with you in six months to see if anything has changed? Maybe it would be a better fit for you at some point in the future.*

Decision: *It looks great, but I have to think about it.*

Inappropriate response: *What's to think about? You just said it looks great. The sooner you get in, the better it is for you.*

Appropriate response: *No problem. Is there anything we haven't addressed adequately, any additional information you need in order to make a decision? (No.) Okay, good. Can you tell us how much time you think you need and when we should contact you? We're doing several appointments and enrolling new people this week, so knowing when to get back with you will help us coordinate our schedule.*

Overselling is a frequent mistake made by inexperienced network marketers. Pressuring people is worse yet. It tells the prospect that you are desperate or self-centered, or both. A decision is a decision. It is closure, at least for that moment. Don't continue to sell and don't pressure people.

Some network marketers argue that you should presume that every prospect will sign up after the presentation. They say you should not ask the prospect *if* they want to join, but rather *how* they want to join—either as a customer or business owner. Be careful framing a decision for your prospects in that way. While most people may not have a problem with this approach, some will be offended by your presumption.

Bring Help

If you are a new network marketer, we strongly recommend that you have your upline do the appointment for you. In this case, your job is very simple. First, you introduce your prospect to your upline. Second, you tell your story when your upline asks you to do so. That's it.

And, when we say "that's it," *that is it!* Don't try to co-present, don't interrupt your upline and don't answer when your upline asks your prospect a question. This will only confuse the prospect. It will also ruin the connection your upline is making with your prospect. This would be a good time to open a bottle of *Shut Up* and take a big drink from it.

As your upline finishes the presentation and proceeds to ask for a decision, you may get antsy. These can be tense moments for new network marketers. Remain calm and quiet. Give the prospect as much time as she or he needs to think and respond. Let your upline handle the conversation after the prospect responds.

This is not about taking control away from you or shutting you out of the process. Take yourself and your feelings out of it. This is about the prospect and what is best for them. Trust the knowledge and experience of your upline.

In-Home Presentations

Giving presentations in your home can be appealing to your prospects, as they add a social dynamic to the appointment. In-home presentations are typically a good fit for your family and close friends. Be sure to keep the number of guests manageable so that the room does not become crowded.

Ask that people RSVP. A few days before the event, call your guests who have said they are coming and confirm that they still plan to attend. Call those who have not sent an RSVP to see if they would still like to come. Keep in mind that not everyone who says they are coming will actually turn up. Even some of those who promise and sound excited when you talk to them will not show. Don't let it discourage you. It happens to everyone in this business. That's just how it goes.

Though the evening may have a strong social element, you want it to remain professional. If you have small children, consider having your spouse or a friend take them out for the evening. If you have pets, keep them confined to another area of the house.

In-home presentations typically result in a high percentage of guests placing orders or enrolling, so be prepared with all of the proper forms.

Opportunity Meetings

Opportunity meetings, which are presentations made to a large number of people, can be very powerful. These meetings are also often called "open meetings" because they are open to the public. These may be weekly, monthly or quarterly depending on how your business operates. Opportunity meetings have significant advantages over in-home presentations and personal appointments:

1) They are typically held in a professional environment, such as a business suite or hotel conference room, giving your opportunity substantial credibility. *Nice place. These people are serious about what they do.*

2) They create a higher level of excitement and anticipation. *Look at this crowd; something exciting must be happening!*

3) They produce a sense of urgency among the guests. *If there are this many people excited about this, I don't want to miss out on it!*

4) They validate the opportunity by showing a much larger picture. *Honey, did you hear all of those testimonials tonight? It sounds like this is for real.*

5) They give you the ability to personally introduce your prospect to several leaders at one time. *These people are successful; I'm impressed. If they're helping me, I think I can do this.*

Remember, the more you can remove yourself from the process and show your opportunity through other people, the better. Open meetings are a great way to do this.

After The Appointment

If your prospect has said "Yes" or "Maybe" to your opportunity, set a date and time for your next contact before the two of you part company.

Always strive to have the next appointment set before the current one ends. Just as you did when making your initial contact, impress upon her that she should write the appointment in her calendar and to call you if she cannot be available for your next meeting or phone call.

If her decision about the business is "No," ask if you can contact her in six months to see if her feelings have changed. If she is agreeable, record that in your notes. If she declines, note that as well and do not call her again. Honor her wishes.

Get out your journal again and write down anything else noteworthy. Does she have any concerns or objections? Any specific questions? If so, what are they? Then, be sure to address these during your next contact with her.

Record which upline you brought into the conversation. This way, you will know to introduce her to a different person next time. How embarrassing it is to get your upline on the phone with a prospect a second time without realizing it. *That was a nice story, but it was the same guy you had me talk to last time.* Oops!

Each time your prospect is exposed to your opportunity, whether it is a one-on-one presentation, open meeting, in-home group presentation or conference call, remember to take good notes. This will help you avoid awkward moments like the one we just described, and will also help you plan the next phase of the process: follow-up.

That we will discuss next.

Quick Review: The Presentation

1) Your top priority on an appointment is to LISTEN and ASK QUESTIONS.
2) You don't have to be perfect, just sincere.
3) Talk about benefits, not features.
4) Use your prospect's Need or Dream to illustrate your compensation plan.
5) Present your opportunity as a solution to their problem.
6) Always ask for a decision. Then, respect that decision.
7) Bring upline support to the presentation.
8) Make notes during and after the presentation.

Exercise

1) During your appointment with Henri, he confides in you that his company has to lay off 20 percent of its workforce due to lagging sales. He has been with the company for 15 years, but despite his seniority he will lose his job in 60 days. Ask your sponsor or another upline to role play with you. They will play the part of Henri. What would you say to him? Remember to validate his fears and try to use a story that ties his needs to your opportunity.

2) Cheryl is an instructor at a tennis facility. She gives individual lessons and also conducts clinics for groups of people wanting to learn how to play tennis. Again, have your sponsor or another upline role play with you. They will be Cheryl and you will demonstrate your company's compensation plan using Cheryl's profession as your example. (You may want to review the section on Tom the truck dispatcher.)

3) You just finished your presentation to Lisa. It is time to ask for a decision. Have your upline play the part of Lisa. Role play two scenarios, one in which Lisa is open to the business opportunity and one in which she is not. In each case, how do you respond to Lisa's decision?

SIX

Follow-Up

Mary has just had a fantastic appointment with Jan. During their time together, Jan confided that she has been praying for an answer to their financial problems. It has been a difficult couple of years. Her husband, Phil, has been laid off and at age 52 is finding it impossible to find another job. They struggle to meet their monthly obligations, often resorting to credit cards. As they part company, Jan says, "Mary, thank you so much. I believe this is the answer to a prayer. I really want to do this business."

Mary is so excited, she can barely stand it. How wonderful it is to have someone who truly appreciates the opportunity and is motivated to make a change in life. Mary is deeply touched by Jan's situation and can't wait to pour herself into helping Jan and her family.

Mary immediately calls her husband to tell him the great news. "Honey, I just had the best appointment; I think I've found a runner," she tells him. "We need to go out to dinner and celebrate!"

Mary greets the next day brimming with anticipation, certain that Jan will be calling to get her business started. When Jan doesn't call, Mary is sure it is because she was busy and didn't have time. "She'll call tomorrow," she tells herself, reassuringly.

A week goes by and there is no word from Jan. Mary is worried. What if something happened? What if she was in an accident? She calls Jan. No answer. She leaves a message. Another week goes by, and Mary leaves another voicemail. The messages go unreturned; Mary never hears from Jan again.

Mary is crushed. "How could this happen?" she wonders. "Jan was so excited. I don't get it. Why does this business have to be so hard?"

Sound familiar? Unfortunately, this is a scenario that plays out over and over and over again. What Mary has failed to recognize is that after their appointment, something happens to Jan:

LIFE. Life happens.

Jan goes home and tells her husband, Phil, all about the business opportunity and how excited she is. He shrugs. "I don't know," Phil says. "Is it one of those pyramid things? We can't afford to be throwing money away, especially now."

Jan's mom calls. Jan's dad has fallen and needs to go to the emergency room. Jan rushes over to her parents' house to help. When she gets home, her daughter reminds Jan that she doesn't have what she needs for her school project. Can they go shopping in the morning?

As Jan crawls into bed after midnight, she says to herself, "I don't have even one extra minute in my day. How could I possibly start a business?"

The next day, Jan talks to her friend, Lois, about everything that's going on: her husband still out of work, her dad in the hospital, her daughter needing things that they don't have money for. She tells Lois about the business appointment she had a few days ago.

"Oh, Jan," says Lois. "You don't actually buy that 'get rich' stuff, do you? My sister tried one of those things and never made a dime. Aren't there some part-time jobs you could take?"

Jan hangs up the phone as Phil walks into the room. "The kitchen ceiling is leaking," he says.

Jan sighs. "Great, that's all we need!"

The following week, Phil finds a temporary job. For at least a little while, they will have some breathing room. Life feels normal again, almost. "It's not so bad after all," Jan tells herself. "Lois is probably right. What was I thinking, anyway?" She doesn't give her appointment with Mary another thought.

There is an important lesson to be learned here: your business will languish if, like Mary, you wait for people to call you back. *You* have to follow up with them; *you* have to take the initiative. Don't fool yourself into believing that the prospect is going to call you or chase you down to join your business. It almost never happens!

We are all busy and all creatures of routine. Our lives become a rut that is hard to escape. Don't expect your prospects to get out of the rut by themselves. If they could do it without you, they would have done it by now.

Understand that a gap exists between *seeing* an opportunity and *believing* an opportunity. Yes, they are excited during your appointment and everything you said makes sense, but they have not had enough exposure to your opportunity to really believe in it. Not yet. You need to help them believe it. *You* need to show them more, *you* need to take the lead, *you* need to fill the gap!

The Emotion Factor

Before we explain how to do proper follow-up, let's take a closer look at how human beings make decisions. In particular, we need to look at situations that cause us worry or pain, or present a dilemma of some kind.

When we have a significant need in our lives, our response to that need is highly emotional. Emotions often spill out in what we think, say and do. Being treated unfairly at work can make us irritable; we start arguing with our spouse or yelling at the kids over simple things. A serious health issue can cause us to be depressed; we withdraw, not wanting to leave the house or talk to anyone. When we don't have enough money for our bills, we develop anxiety; we become fearful and lose sleep.

So, when someone shows us a possible solution to our problems, our immediate thoughts, words and actions are very much an emotional response. We begin to feel hopeful, optimistic, even joyful. *What if this is what I've been looking for? Could this be my answer?*

This is why testimonials are so powerful and why you need to make sure your prospect hears a lot of them. When he sees how other people have come from similar circumstances and made drastic improvements in *their* lives, it helps him connect the business opportunity to *his* life. He sees the opportunity from *his* perspective. The importance of testimonials cannot be overstated; they are the currency of this business. It's the experiences of others that give the prospect hope, and start him down the path to taking ownership of the opportunity.

The Logic Factor

While emotions play a huge role in how we make decisions, wise decisions are never made on emotion alone. Emotion may bring someone to the table, but it won't keep them there. There has to be more. The decision must also be *logical;* it has to make sense. This is the validation test. Your prospect has a need to know that the opportunity is genuine, that there is substance beyond the emotional appeal. *This sounds too good to be true* is your cue that he is looking for validation.

Logic questions include the following:

Are people actually making money in this business?

Do the marketing plan and business model make sense?

Are the products and services marketable? Do they work?

How stable is the company? What is its history?

Are the company leaders competent and trustworthy?

Is the support team (the upline) adequately skilled?

How experienced are they?

What marketing tools are used in this business?

Is there training and if so, how does it work?

Advancing The Prospect

As we explained earlier, the purpose of your presentation is to help people connect their Dream to your opportunity, to get them "possibility thinking." The subsequent Follow-Up step is every bit as important as the Invitation and Presentation steps. Remember, your presentation is just one exposure and is usually not sufficient for your prospect to make an informed decision.

First and foremost, follow-up protects the prospect's Dream. Jan's Dream died because of the negative and distracting influences of everyday life. And, Mary did nothing to prevent it. Just like Jan, your prospects will encounter: 1) their own doubt—*How could I possibly start a business? I've never done anything like that;* and, 2) the ignorance of others, disguised as wise counsel—*You don't actually buy that "get rich" stuff, do you?*

A second purpose of follow-up is to "advance" the prospect. You want to advance her down the road toward a decision. With each follow-up contact, you are presenting both emotional and logical input that your prospect will use to make a decision.

The purpose of follow-up is to inform the prospect's mind, not make up her mind or change her mind. Do not attempt to convince or manipulate a "No" into a "Yes." There is a clear difference between convincing and advancing and you must be careful to not cross the line.

And, if your prospect signs up during your appointment, you still need to do follow-up. Getting in doesn't necessarily mean *staying* in. Remember: LIFE HAPPENS.

How To Do Proper Follow-Up

Now that we've covered why you need to do good follow-up, let's examine *how* you do it. We have stressed several times the importance of keeping good notes each time you speak with your prospects. You will need to refer to those notes to determine the best way to advance them. (Ask your upline for input.)

Let's suppose that you are reviewing your notes on Scott. Your notes so far read:

Jan. 7 – initial telephone call; Scott says he is not really looking for a business; he's really busy—can I just tell him in one minute what this is all about?; told him that this deserves more than one minute; why not meet me for lunch— you have to eat anyway; insists he's not interested but agrees to meet; appointment set for tomorrow, Noon at Bailey's Deli.

Jan. 8 – lunch at Bailey's; Scott looks tired and I ask him why; he's been working 70-hour weeks; the store is down two sales associates and as manager, he has to take up the slack plus do his own work;

    Owner said it would be temporary but it's going on 12 months with no new hires; Scott thinks the owner is just trying to save money; he has worked 48 of the last 50 days;

    Had a fight with his fiancée, Amanda, over missing Christmas at her parents' house; showed him the marketing plan, which he said makes sense but how could he fit one more thing into his life?; told him I know someone who could answer that question better than I can;

He's still only mildly interested at best, but agreed to learn more; 3-way call with Shawn scheduled for tomorrow at Noon; shared appointment highlights with Shawn.

Jan. 9 – Scott not there at scheduled time, left him a voice mail; he called back later and apologized; had to work through lunch to cover for sick employee; rescheduled for 10:30pm tonight; had him talk to Shawn this evening;

Notes from Shawn's discussion with Scott:

Scott, are you living the life you want? (No);

Tell me about your life; What's going on with you? (Scott tells Shawn the same story he told me);

Scott, I was going down the same path as you when I was your age... (Shawn shares his business story); If I hadn't taken control of my life at that point, my wife would have probably been going to Christmas dinner alone, just like Amanda;

Do you and Amanda plan on having kids? (Yes);

Is this the life you want for them? (No);

If you don't make a change, Scott, how will your life be any different in one year? 5 years? 10 years? (I don't know; hadn't thought about it until now);

Do you think you owe it to yourself and Amanda—and, especially the children you will have some day—to plan your life instead of just letting it happen to you? (Now that you put it that way, Yes. I guess I hadn't really considered it.)

Scott, do you have time to look at an opportunity that could change your future? (I'll make time.)

Invited Scott to open meeting on Jan. 11; Scott has to work that night; there is a conference call tomorrow but it's not until 11pm local time; no problem, Scott says he should be available.

Let's review everything you have done thus far:

    1) During your initial contact, you politely declined Scott's request for detailed information;

2) You set the appointment;

3) You learned a great deal about Scott's situation during the presentation;

4) You turned his objection about being too busy into an opportunity to introduce your upline;

5) You connected Scott to Shawn and remained quiet while Shawn built a rapport with him;

6) You set the next appointment before ending the current conversation.

You are doing a fantastic job of advancing Scott! Your goal now is to continue to show Scott more and more of your opportunity. It's important that you include his fiancée, Amanda, as soon as possible. Because of his schedule, you haven't been able to do this yet. However, your upline is having a get-together at their house this weekend. The kids will be snow sledding while the adults play billiards and foosball and visit by the fire.

You invite Scott and Amanda. As it turns out, he has the day off; they can come. In fact, Amanda was just lamenting that they never get to go out and do fun things like they used to before Scott was promoted to manager. They are looking forward to coming.

That weekend, Scott and Amanda meet their future support team. They are impressed with how genuine, friendly, humble and wise your friends are. It is an incredibly positive and hopeful atmosphere. They see the lifestyle that is attainable and leave excited about the possibilities.

You invite them to next week's open meeting. Scott cannot attend— he is working again—but Amanda will be there. There is a conference call on Monday night at 9:00 p.m. You suggest they join you. Amanda is available. Scott won't be home until almost 9:30 but he will call in on his cell phone as he is driving home.

You talk to them immediately after the conference call. They are extremely excited. You tell them to be thinking of people who need to hear about the opportunity and to start putting names on paper. You remind Amanda of the open meeting tomorrow night and confirm that she is attending. She says she will be there. Scott announces that he was able to get someone to cover for him and he will be there, too!

The night of the meeting they both sign up. You tell them about a business training Saturday at 9:30 a.m. Amanda will be there. Scott has to be at work by 11 a.m. but will come for the first hour. They are off to a great start.

Will every scenario play out this well when you do good follow-up? Unfortunately, no. There will be many, many times when despite your excellent follow-up, your prospect will say "No" to the opportunity, will skip their appointment with you and not bother to call, will be a no-show at an open meeting and will ignore your phone calls. That's just the way the business works. You will only sponsor a few of the people you talk to and only some of *them* will develop into business leaders.

But, think for a moment about what resulted from your follow-up with Scott. Initially he was resistant, thinking he was way too busy. Now, he and Amanda are excited and dreaming about a life they never thought they could have. What if you would have answered Scott's questions on that initial call? What if after the appointment, when Scott was only faintly interested, you would have waited for him to call you back? Don't you think this scenario would have turned out much differently? You bet! Scott and Amanda wouldn't have the chance at a better future that they now have. Instead, they would likely be starting off their life together under a lot of stress and uncertainty.

That is the power of follow-up. When done properly, follow-up builds a mountain of undeniable evidence and fans the flame of possibility thinking.

Advancing The Dream

Now that Scott and Amanda have joined the business, your work is done, right? They will start building a huge business and you can move on to the next prospect; isn't that so?

No.

Some network marketers, particularly those who are new in the business, have the mistaken notion that all they need to do is sign people up and the rest of the business will happen on its own. Even some people who have been in the business a long time do this; they sponsor, but the people they bring in never seem to do much of anything.

Why does this happen? Most of the time the problem is us: we fail to see that sponsoring is the not the end, it is just the beginning. Our work really starts *after* someone signs up.

Scott and Amanda are no longer prospects—they have joined the business—but you need to continue to advance them, nonetheless. The only difference is that now you are advancing *their Dream.* They responded to the opportunity emotionally, you validated the business logically and they signed up. Now, you have to take it a step further. You must transfer the opportunity *visually.* You must help them envision their Dream.

The Visualization Factor

You must become a visionary. You must develop an ability to see things before they happen, to see into the future. Moreover, you need to help your downline visualize *their* future. Help them see and feel what it will be like when they are living their Dream.

Why is it so important for us to visualize our Dream? Because there will be times in this business when the Dream is all we have. There will be stretches where nothing goes right and we want to quit. It is in these moments that the Dream sees us through.

It might be tough right now and I might feel like giving up, but I am not going to because I have my Dream! I know what I want and I know how to get it. I already know what it will look and feel like when I achieve it. I am not going to stop now!

The most powerful thing you can do to help your downline catch a vision of their Dream is to paint them a picture of what it is like to already possess that which they are pursuing: financial independence, time freedom, a greater sense of purpose. If their Dream is to be home with their children, introduce them to someone in your upline who is living it. Have the upline person tell them what it means to her and to her children to be able to spend that time together. What memories are they creating that they otherwise wouldn't be? What values is she able to model for her children that she couldn't before?

If your new downline wants total time and financial freedom, introduce him to someone in your upline who has it. Let him get a taste of it. That's exactly what someone did for Dave Bradley, who recalls this defining moment:

Early on in my business, I had the opportunity to spend the day with a group of businessmen, each of whom had built a very large organization with my company. One of them had a boat and I was among the people who were invited to spend the day out on the water. At this point in my life I was not yet financially independent and jumped at the chance to spend time with people who were. I wanted to learn from them, just be around them.

We had a fantastic time, relaxing in the bright sunshine, talking, laughing, eating and taking in the sights. *I could get used to this,* I thought.

A man named Tim struck up a conversation with me. "Did you get the day off work?" he asked.

"Yes, I did," I replied. It was a beautiful weekday and I didn't have to go to the office. It was a rare treat.

"When you drove into the marina early this morning, did you notice the traffic?"

"I sure did," I said. The motorway had been full of cars, four lanes across.

"What direction were they going?" he asked me.

"They were headed toward downtown; going to work, I suppose," I replied.

"And, which direction were *you* going?" he asked. It was clear that he was making a point.

"I was going the other way," I answered.

"Right," he said. "They were going to work, just like they do every day and will for the rest of their lives. You, however, were going the other way. And, now you have a taste of what it's like to be free.

"By the way," he added, "the traffic was pretty light heading this direction, wasn't it?"

"It sure was!" I said with a laugh.

I have never forgotten that day. The picture he painted while we sat on that boat is burned into me. It stayed with me as I built my business. When I got frustrated and wanted to slow down or felt like giving up, the image of those cars on the motorway—the people inside them heading to their jobs—kept me going. I had a Dream and I was determined to be the guy heading in a different direction.

Ginny Fiscella believes your Dream should be the last thing you see when you go to bed at night, that you should fall asleep with your head on your Dream. And, that's literally what she teaches to her group:

> We do what we call "dream pillow cases." We get together and everyone gets a white pillow case and permanent markers and I tell them to draw what they want their business to bring them from that day into the future.
>
> I will never forget what happened for Marnie Cole. Marnie originally started this business because she wanted to buy new rugs for her kitchen. But, as we would do these Dream sessions it would cause us—not just Marnie, all of us—to begin to broaden our vision.
>
> Well, Marnie drew a cabin on her pillow case. She had always wanted a lake house for her and her children to be able to go to on the weekends. And, here is the power in doing these kinds of things: five years later, she was able to buy that house! In fact, we had that pillow case framed and it's now hanging on the wall in her lake house.
>
> I always tell my people, "Picture it, sleep on it and dream away. And, when your Dream comes true, we will frame it for you."

What powerful imagery! In both of these examples, the focus was not on business strategy or marketing techniques. These activities were about fun and relaxation…and dream building. Tim and Ginny used imagery—a crowded highway, a pillow case—to illustrate the Dream. They understand that it is not enough for people to connect to their Dream emotionally and logically; they must also connect to it *visually*.

We all dream in pictures. Strive to give your downline a picture of their Dream they will never forget.

Get Them Off To A Solid Start

The first days following a new network marketer's enrollment are critical to her long-term success. If she can have some early positive results, this will give her confidence and establish important momentum in her business. Like the blacksmith working a piece of iron right out of the fire, you should act while the new networkers' excitement is burning. You have to "strike while the iron is hot" for her to get off to a solid start.

Arrange a meeting with her—preferably in person, but if necessary on the phone—within 24 hours after she enrolls. If that is not possible, schedule the meeting at her first availability, hopefully within 48 hours. We can tell you from experience that when new networkers do not start taking action immediately, they struggle or never start at all.

Remember that the naysayers of the world and their own doubts and fears will be trying to steal their Dream. Some will be easily distracted. Others may have a "never-in-a-hurry" personality. Do your best to convey a sense of urgency, but realize that some people will just sit at the starting gate. Ultimately it's up to them, not you.

Develop A Checklist

We do not believe in excessive forms and paperwork; the more of these you have, the more you complicate your business. And, the more you complicate things the harder they are for people to do. The simpler it is, the better.

That said, having a few forms will actually make things easier for you. For instance, you should consider having a Beginner's Checklist. Any time we are trying to learn something new, whether it is starting a business or programming a cell phone, step-by-step instructions come in handy. Most of us are well accustomed to ticking off tasks as we complete them.

The checklist can be a comfort to you when you are new in this business. In the beginning, you may feel overwhelmed. Having a document to refer to that outlines everything you need to do will help you learn the business more quickly, and this will boost your confidence. Naturally, we don't want a checklist to replace relationships. Be sure to stay in close contact with your upline.

A checklist also introduces you to two very important concepts: *accountability* and *duplication*. When an item on the checklist is completed, it is crossed off the list. There is no mistaking whether the task is done or undone. It's right there on paper, in black and white. You are accountable for completing each of the steps.

When you complete the tasks and see some success in your business (or at a minimum see the logic of the process), what will you likely teach the people you sponsor? *The very same thing.* You will teach them to use the checklist. Now, you have duplication taking place.

Here are the basic elements of a checklist to help new network marketers get their businesses started:

1) *List of Contacts* – This should top the list. Start making your list immediately. You can't start a business without invested capital, and this is your capital. Review the list with your upline as we suggested in the chapter on Stream of Contacts, discussing key people on your list.

2) *Set Appointments* – Strike while the iron is hot. Set appointments within 48 hours of your enrollment. Don't let your excitement burn out!

3) *Your WHY (the Dream)* – Your WHY is your reason for doing the business. Write down not only what you want but *why* you want it. *When* do you want it? *Who* benefits from your Dream (in addition to you)? *How* do you expect to accomplish the Dream? (What excuses are you willing to give up? What obstacles will you have to overcome? How badly do you want it?)

4) *Logistics* – Ask your upline to teach you how to fill out the appropriate business application and other forms. They should do it with you but not *for* you. The same goes for ordering product for yourself and your customers. You will need to learn this very quickly, but note that we did not make it No. 1 on the list. Never put the emphasis on the business of doing the business. Instead, keep the focus on the Dream and talking to people.

5) *Relationship Building* – Take ample time to get acquainted with your upline as well as everyone you sponsor. Anyone you have brought into the business should already be connected to your upline if you've done things properly. Now, you need to continue to build those relationships. You will all be working together and need to develop a rapport and mutual trust. You are a networker

and a network is simply a group of relationships; build the relationships and you will build the business.

6) *Goals / Plan of Action* – Most people don't know how to set business goals, or even that they should be doing it. Again, your upline should do this with you but not *for* you. You have to make your own goals. It is not critical that this is done in the first couple of days, but don't let it linger.

7) *Training* – Plug into your standard training as quickly as possible. You will need to learn how to explain the company's products and services. You will need to learn how to present the marketing plan. Group training is preferable to one-on-one; having several trainees together adds excitement and encourages creativity.

8) *Modeling* – You will learn more by what you are shown than by what you are told. Ask your upline to model the business for you. Role-play with them the Invitation Step, active listening and how to ask for a decision. Ask them to join you on your initial appointments. Observe closely how they present the company, the products and the marketing plan.

   Dial in to a conference call that they are hosting and listen to how they lead the call. Ask to join them on a follow-up call they are doing with one of their prospects. Not only will you learn, it will also help your upline. By having you, a new networker, on the phone it shows the prospect the training and mentoring that will be there for her when *she* joins the business.

9) *Personal Development Program* – Fear, doubt, discouragement, lack of focus—everyone who starts a business will have these and many more hurdles to clear. That is why we strongly recommend that you have an ongoing Personal Development Program (PDP). Having a PDP isn't just a good idea; it is essential. Take advantage of books and audio resources that will strengthen your self-confidence, communication skills and leadership abilities. Your upline will likely have many suggested selections for you.

10) *Dream Building* – We should always be building the Dream no matter how long we've been in the business. But, it is even more important for the networker who is brand new. Look for

opportunities to participate in dream-building activities, such as those Dave and Ginny describe. The more focused you are on your Dream, the more likely your upline will look to include you in these events. Keep the fire burning. No Dream, no steam.

If you have a downline, it is appropriate for you to initiate some of the items on the checklist for them, such as the relationship and dream building. You should also make suggestions regarding the personal development piece. However, do not complete the checklist for your downline; they need to do it themselves. It is their business and they need to be responsible for it. As with everything, do it with them but not *for* them.

Quick Review: Follow-Up

1) Don't wait for prospects to call you back. You need to call *them*.

2) Always set the next appointment before your current conversation ends.

3) Your goal is to advance the prospect toward a decision.

4) We respond to opportunities emotionally, logically and visually. Effective follow-up addresses each of these.

5) Follow-up does not end when your prospect signs up. In fact, your job has just begun. Advance the Dream!

6) Use a checklist to help you learn and get off to a fast start.

Exercise

1) Think about a time in your business that you didn't do proper follow-up. What could you have done better? What kept you from following through? Was it fear? Lack of discipline? Did you pre-judge the prospect? What did you learn from that experience?

2) Describe a time in your business when you were able to visualize your Dream. This may have been through your own imagination. It may have been through another person, as in the example of Dave Bradley. Or, perhaps it was a dream-building activity like the one Ginny Fiscella shared.

Getting Them Started

1) List of Contacts   Date Completed

   Do immediately   _____

   Review with upline   _____

2) Set Appointments

   First appt. within 48 hours   _____

   5 appts. within 10 days   _____

3) Your WHY (the Dream)

WHY are you doing this business?

   What do you want?   _____

   When do you want it?   _____

   Who benefits from it?   _____

   How will you accomplish it?_____

4) Logistics

   Application / Registration   _____

   Order products   _____

5) Relationship Building

   Meet upline support team   _____

   Social event with the group_____

6) Goals / Plan of Action

   Written goals   _____

   Plan of action   _____

   Discuss with upline _____

7) Training   Date Completed

   Learn the products   _____

   Learn the marketing plan _____

8) Modeling

   Joint presentation w/upline _____

   3-way call (follow-up)   _____

   Role play: invitation step _____

   Role play: active listening _____

   Role play: ask for decision _____

9) Personal Development Program (PDP)

   1st book / video / audio   _____

   2nd book / video / audio   _____

   3rd book / video / audio   _____

   4th book / video / audio   _____

   5th book / video / audio   _____

10) Dream Building

   Dream Building Exercise 1 _____

   Dream Building Exercise 2 _____

SEVEN

Prospecting

As you build your business, you will encounter people of varying backgrounds: those with means and those without; those with positive attitudes and those with rotten attitudes; those who are hungry for more in their lives and those who fear change of any kind. Some people are great candidates for your business opportunity; others are not and never will be.

So, how do you navigate your business through the attitudes, motives, experiences, fears, beliefs and objections of the people you invite to look at your opportunity? You do it through a process known as "prospecting."

Prospecting is simply the process of finding out what people want, whether or not they are willing to work for it and whether or not your opportunity is the right vehicle. *Do they want more out of life? What are they willing to do to get it? Do they see your business as a way to get it?* That's prospecting.

A Sorting Process

This business would be much easier if people wore signs that said "Looking for a home-based business." Unfortunately, it doesn't happen that way. Instead, we have to go looking for people. Network marketing is essentially a sorting process. That's what it boils down to: sorting. It's like any card game. The way to win the game is to collect certain cards. You accomplish this by drawing from the deck, holding onto the valuable cards and discarding those that won't help you win.

Prospecting works the same way. You are looking for the "royalty" in the deck: the Aces, Kings and Queens. These are the people who want what you have to offer. But to find the valuable cards, you will have to sort through the rest, including the Jokers. The day you start your business, everyone is an "unknown." All of the cards are face down and thus all look the same. Every card is a "Yes" or a "No" waiting to be turned over, identified and sorted. You hold onto each "Yes" and discard each "No."

Can you control where the leaders are placed in the deck? No, you cannot. Your leaders may be in the middle of the deck while the next network marketer will find them at the top. You can't worry about that. Instead, worry about the things that you *can* control. You control how many people you talk to each day, and therefore how many decks you can sort in a week, a month or a year. You control the rate of the personal development required for you to overcome your fears. You control how skilled you become at leadership and attracting others to your opportunity.

If you are like everyone else in this business, you weren't wearing a sign, either. In fact, you may not have even considered network marketing until someone showed you the opportunity. The person who introduced you to network marketing had to show you the possibilities, had to paint you a picture. Now, your job is to do the same for others.

Maybe you don't think you can do that. Maybe you don't believe there are still people out there who will say "Yes" to your opportunity. Perhaps you think that it's too late, that all of the Aces are gone from the deck. If that is where you are right now, just remember that there are already thousands (or tens of thousands) of networkers in your company. If there are that many people excited about your business, don't you suppose you can find some more? Trust us: there are plenty of Aces still in the deck!

Four Types of People

You will encounter four types of people as you build your business:

1) People who do NOT want what you have and are NOT going to want it in the future;

2) People who do NOT want what you have, but only because NOW is not the right time;

3) People who say YES to what you have BUT can't or won't do what is necessary to have it;

4) People who say YES to what you have and WILL do what it takes to have it.

Let's call these four types of people the Not-Nots, the Not-Nows, the Yes-Buts and the Yes-Wills.

The NOT-NOTs

Many people are completely happy with their lives and wouldn't dream of doing anything else. They were born to do what they are doing and intend to do it for the rest of their days. You can't help them achieve their Dream because they are already living it. When you encounter these people, congratulate them and move on. They are not prospects.

The other segment of the Not-Not population is the people who don't want the business and you don't want *them*. These are the people on your "turkey list," the ones you do not respect and thus try to avoid. They are negative and their problems are everybody else's fault and never their own. Likewise, these people are not prospects.

The NOT-NOWs

These people are right for your business but the timing is not right for them. Make a note of their present situation and the date you talked to them. Put them in your "parking lot," the spot in your notebook reserved for people you intend to contact again in the future. Ask permission to call the Not-Nows periodically to see if their situation has changed. At some point in their life, they may want and need what you have.

The YES-BUTs

Some people want what you have but are not willing to work for it. *Yes*, they want the lifestyle, *but* won't make the sacrifice. *Yes*, they want the baby *but* without the labor. They will join the business but find excuses not to be disciplined and persistent. They won't invest in themselves to develop necessary skills. The YES-BUTs are a roll of the dice. Be careful how much time you invest in them.

THE YES-WILLs

These are the people who seize your opportunity and are willing to work for their Dream. The Yes-Wills are leaders and they self-identify. They are the ones calling you for help, asking questions, seeking your advice. When the phone rings and you see it's them calling, you always answer. You look forward to talking to them because you know they have a hunger and a determination. Give of yourself generously to the Yes-Wills; you are making a great investment.

People Will Say No To Your Opportunity

You have a product that helps people have better health, improves the look of their skin, provides healthier drinking water, saves them money on utility bills, provides quality legal protection or helps them look their best and feel more self-confident. You have a great product, yet many people will tell you, "No."

You have a business opportunity that can give people relief from a job loss or other financial crisis, help them prepare for retirement, give them financial freedom, time freedom and a greater sense of purpose. Yet, people will tell you, "No."

Many of them will be friends and family. Often, it's the people we are closest to who not only say "No," but think they have a license to be insensitive (or even cruel) about it.

Such is the nature of the business. *Not every person you talk to is a prospect.* Some people truly love what they do and wouldn't dream of doing anything but their current job or business. Others hate what they do but would rather put up with it than make a change. Get used to the fact that most people will tell you, "No." Understand that the reason is not you. Never take it personally. People are saying "No" to the opportunity, not rejecting you.

Just remember that what you have to offer is an opportunity, not a guarantee. What you have can be a true blessing to people, but first they have to want it.

Quality Vs. Quantity

In this business, quality trumps quantity every time. It is far better to have a few good people in your downline who are hungry than a hundred who do nothing. However, for your business to have quality people, you have to talk to a large quantity of people.

New network marketers are often shocked when they find out what it really takes to build the business. You will have to talk to a lot of people—in some cases hundreds—to sponsor several dozen out of which you may end up with a handful of leaders. Most people aren't prepared for that, particularly the fact that 95 percent or more of the people they sponsor will never build a business. These ratios are just a generalization, not hard science. But, you get the point.

You can't control the quality of the next person you talk to, but you can control the quantity of people you talk to; be prepared to show your opportunity to A LOT of people. You will find your leaders.

Don't Pre-Judge!

Don't categorize people before you talk to them and don't assume what they want and don't want. The old adage remains true: you can't judge a book by its cover. The ultra-successful businessperson, whom you think would never consider your opportunity, might desperately want to get out of the corporate rat race. The seemingly meek and mild-mannered lady in the plain dress and sensible shoes might be a tiger yet to be unleashed. Yes, a first impression is important but it's not always indicative of what's below the surface. Talk to people. Get to know them. Find out what inspires them.

Also remember that ability is not everything. Some people are sharp but not hungry. What good is their ability if they have no desire? Conversely, some people are hungry but not sharp. We may want to discount someone who isn't particularly skilled. But, don't do that! Often, the ones you think are runners will disappoint you and the ones you aren't counting on will surprise you. You can teach someone to become sharp but you cannot teach someone to be hungry.

Look For Success-Minded People

As we go about our prospecting, we tend to look for people who need a way to become successful. Isn't that true? We look for people who are broke, heavily in debt, or have been out of work for months. Our mind says, *"Wow, this person really needs this business."*

That could be true; they might really benefit from this business. But, we shouldn't be looking for people who need a way to be successful. We need to be looking for people who are already "success-minded." Now, success-minded doesn't mean, necessarily, that they currently make a lot of money. It means that regardless of their current financial situation, *success is on their mind.*

People don't suddenly become successful because the right opportunity comes along. Look for people who are already success-minded and hungry for an opportunity.

Qualifying Your Prospect

Most network marketers ask "How do I find people?" when they should really be asking "How do I find the *right* people?"

Let's say that you show your opportunity to a prospect and do a fantastic presentation. You are engaging, empathetic and attentive, you ask all the right questions and do great follow-up. But, when it comes to making a decision your prospect waffles or you can't reach her. She may even join eventually, but then never makes an effort. Have you had that experience? If so, you're in good company; it has happened to all of us!

The problem is that we're often talking to the wrong person, but we just don't realize it. We have failed to qualify our prospect. In other words, we haven't attempted to find out if she is *qualified* to do the business.

WHY YOU QUALIFY PROSPECTS

What do you do when you need a new pair of shoes? You probably go to the store to look for some that meet your qualifications. Even before you walk in the door, you have already made several decisions about the qualities that pair of shoes must have. You know what size you need. You've decided if the shoes will be for work, dress or leisure. You have an idea of how much you are willing to spend. You may even have in mind a particular style, material and color.

You know what you want and you are focused. You do not spend much time with shoes that don't meet your needs. (Well, if you really love shoes this may not be true.) Furthermore, you do not *invest* in shoes that fail to meet your qualifications. You only buy shoes that are "qualified."

If shoes came in a plain brown bag with a label that read SHOES, would you buy them? Of course not! What if they're the wrong size? What if you need steel-toed work boots and inside the bag are house slippers? What if you are going to a formal and inside the bag are tennis shoes? (Okay, for some of us that last one would not be an issue, but you get the point.) We would never buy shoes this way!

But, show us someone in a brown paper bag with a label that says PROSPECT and we will jump at the chance to sign them up. They could have a rotten attitude, no discipline, no ambition and no morals but we overlook all of those warning signs because we're just so excited to have *someone* say "Yes."

If someone is wrong for this business, when would you rather know: now or later? What do you gain by investing your time and effort in the wrong people? There are a lot of people who are going nowhere in life and they don't need your help getting there.

Wouldn't it be better to know right up front whether your prospect is serious about *wanting* what they want or if they are just *wishing* for it? Wouldn't it be better to know up front whether your prospect is motivated to find time for a business or if he just wants to make excuses about how busy he already is? Wouldn't it be better to know now if your prospect is willing and able to make an upfront investment—even if it's a small one—in a business?

In addition to saving you time and effort and reducing your frustration, qualifying your prospects shows them that you are looking for certain people and not just anyone. Ultimately, your prospects will respect you more when you qualify them, regardless of whether or not they join your business.

How You Qualify Prospects

When qualifying a prospect, you are essentially looking for their answer to these two questions:

1) Do they want more than they have now?
2) Are they willing to change their life to have it?

If your prospect is satisfied with his life and does not want more than he has now, STOP. Move on to the next person. Likewise, if the prospect wants more but isn't willing to change his life to get it, STOP. Move on to the next one.

Don't hang on to every prospect, trying to convince them to do the business or hoping that they will somehow "wake up" to the opportunity. Hoping and convincing never work; qualifying always does. The less time you spend with the wrong people, the more time you have to spend with the right ones.

THE INFLUENCE OF FEAR

Many networkers are hesitant to qualify their prospects because they don't want to rule anyone out. And, the reason they don't want to rule anyone out is usually rooted in fear. It took all the courage they could muster just to talk to this *one person*. The quicker they disqualify this prospect, the quicker they have to talk to the next one.

So, in their minds it makes sense to pursue every prospect. They would rather sponsor the wrong people and pray that they somehow become right rather than look for people who are right to begin with. This is what happens when your business operates out of fear instead of strength. When you operate out of strength, you *insist* on qualifying your prospects because you only want to work with the right people. You accept the fact that you will have to talk to hundreds of people to find your leaders.

Take It Away

Human behavior can be an odd thing. Have you ever noticed when little children play how they exert ownership of the things that are theirs? A child may have a doll that she hasn't played with for months, that is sitting at the back of closet or at the bottom of the toy box. She has no interest in it and wouldn't even miss it if it were gone. But, the moment her younger sister picks it up the little girl snatches it from her grasp and says "That's mine!"

Grown-ups are the same way. How many times have you shown your opportunity to a prospect who proceeds to point out what he feels are the drawbacks of your business? He doesn't like this thing or thinks that needs to be improved, or he read something on the Internet; it's just one objection after another. You have offered him a chance to take ownership of his future; you have placed it within his grasp. He has a right to his Dream and you want to help him take it. But, like the doll at the bottom of the toy box, he doesn't want it. In fact, he doesn't even know where his Dream is because he doesn't miss it.

So, what should you do? Try to convince him? Keep educating him until he sees the light? Tell him he's right? No! Absolutely not! Instead, you take it away from him.

Chuck, it is clear to me that my business is not for you and that you are not right for my business, at least right now. I wish you well.

Take it away and walk away. When you do this, Chuck has a decision to make. He can let you walk away or he can say, "Whoa, wait a minute! Maybe I really do need to look at this." In either case, you have done yourself *and Chuck* a favor. If he lets you walk away, he has shown you that this business is not for him (and saved both of you time and frustration). If Chuck says, "Okay, let's talk further," he has shown you that he might have a Dream after all (and thus given you an opportunity to work with him). Sometimes it takes a fear of loss to wake us up.

Remember to maintain your posture and use the take away when necessary. Give your opportunity away freely, but only give it to people who want it. Do you need people for your business? Yes. Do you need any one person? No, you don't.

Handling Objections

We don't like objections, do we? Objections make us anxious. They frustrate us. When people object, we have a tendency to view them as uncooperative. *Why do they have to be that way? Can't they see that what I have can help them?* Objections make us want to stop talking to that person and move on. But, we shouldn't do that. Instead of giving up on people so soon, we should work to turn those objections around. And, doing so requires skill.

First, you should understand that objections are just unanswered questions. The prospect is unsure of something and that uncertainty manifests (comes out of their mouth) as an objection.

Second, you need to turn their statements into questions. If you allow their statement to remain a statement, their brain will "close the door." When the statement is posed as a question, the brain becomes creative. It seeks to answer the question, to find a solution.

Your target is always the unanswered question behind the objection. You want your prospect to have clarity, not an uninformed opinion. Once you have zeroed in on the question, you can address it.

When addressing an objection, never argue, never criticize and never try to convince. Always validate the person's underlying concern. More than anything, people want to be heard and they want their feelings to be respected. You can do this by using a form of response known as Feel-Felt-Found. You acknowledge how the person *feels*, you validate it by saying you once *felt* the same way and then explain that you *found* a reason to think differently.

Here are some common objections and our suggestions for handling them:

You make money off other people

It seems to me that what you are really saying is: *Is it fair and ethical to make money this way?*

I know how you feel. I felt that way, too, when I heard about this. But, then I started thinking about how every time I buy something, someone makes money. When I put gas in the car, when I buy groceries, someone makes money. I finally realized that it's okay to make money if I am providing a product that helps people. I also realized that I'm not making money off the people I sponsor. I am teaching them and mentoring them so that *they* can make money. I have found that I'm not really making money off people, I'm making money because I'm helping them.

Only the few people at the top make any money

I get the feeling that what you're saying is: *I've heard that most people in this business don't make any money. Is that true?*

I can see how you would think that. It's true that not everybody in this business is profitable. But you know what someone explained to me? For the people at the top to get to the top, a lot of people underneath them had to make money, too. They didn't get to the top by the company placing them there; they got there because they worked hard and helped a lot of other people make a lot of money. So, it's not just the people at the top making all the money.

Do you know what else I found? Unlike the corporate world where the person above you always makes more than you, in our business it's not unusual for you to make more than the person who sponsored you and is helping you. How cool is that?!

I READ ABOUT THESE SCAMS ON THE INTERNET

I can see that when you read things like that, it could make you wonder: *Is this company legitimate?*

What I have learned about the Internet is that just because something is posted there doesn't mean it's true. If you look, you will find negative statements about virtually everything on earth. It doesn't mean they are factual.

Do you know what else I learned? Most of the negative things on the web about network marketing companies are actually disguises. If you read (or watch) to the end, the person making those statements will try to sell you something. They know that thousands of people are looking at network marketing to make money and will go to the Internet to do research. So, they write or say the same negative things about dozens of companies, including mine, as a ploy to distract you and to buy whatever it is they are selling instead.

Some people aren't selling anything, but are just mad at the company or mad at their upline—or maybe just mad at life. It doesn't mean the opportunity is a scam.

So, I hear what you are saying and I believe we all need to be careful. I have also learned that it goes both ways: 1) you will read about things on the web that sound too good to be true and really *are* too good to be true; they are scams; and 2) you will also find so-called "warnings" about things that are actually legitimate and a great opportunity.

We all need to be smart and the best way to do that, I have found, is to not rely on just one source for information whether that source is positive or negative. Gather information from many different places and weigh it all together before making a decision.

I WON'T BE PART OF A PYRAMID SCHEME

I think what everyone wants to know is: *Are the bad things I've heard about network marketing true?*

Pyramid schemes are scams and you really need to be careful because they can be pretty convincing. If you are thinking that's what this is, I can understand your confusion. There is a lot of bad information out there about our business. I have found that if you really look for the truth, you will find it. And, I did. I saw that this business is real and it's helping people.

I CAN'T AFFORD TO START A BUSINESS

What I think I hear you saying is: *How much does it cost? Where would I find money to do this?*

I can appreciate that. Most people these days don't have any extra money at all. You know, there are a lot of advantages of our business model over traditional businesses. One of the big advantages is that it takes very little money to get started. And, a lot of people are able to recoup their investment and have a debt-free business very quickly.

I DON'T HAVE TIME

It seems to me that what you are really saying is: *How could I possibly fit one more thing into my schedule?*

I hear you! I haven't met many people lately who have much free time to do anything. I didn't think I had time, either. But, you know what? I knew that if I didn't change my life, my life wasn't going to change. I believe that if we really want something in life, we will find the time for it. And, you know what I have found? In this business, it's not so much the amount of time that is important but what we do with the time we have.

The products are expensive

It's a question of value, right? *How do I know these products are really worth it?*

You know, if I was considering just the price of the products I might think the same thing. I have found, though, that the real issue is value, not cost. If something works, it is worth paying for, right? How many times do we spend money on something that doesn't cost much, but also does nothing for us? In the end what's really important is the value we get from the product, not its cost. Wouldn't you agree?

I don't know anyone

Two questions that most people have are: *1) How do you find people? and 2) What do you say?*

I know how you feel. When I started, I didn't think I knew anyone. You know what? I found that I really knew more people than I thought I did. I also found that if you just listen to people, they will reveal that they have a need and all you have to do is offer to help with that need. A lot of this business is just listening and acting on what you hear.

The market is saturated

What I hear you saying is: *Is there enough of a market available for me to build a business?*

You know, given that network marketing has been around for decades, I can see why you might think that. Makes sense. But, guess what I learned? Network marketing is still growing after all these years. And, the untapped market is actually huge. I didn't realize that network marketing accounts for less than one percent of total annual retail sales in the United States. *Less than one percent!* So, if you think about it network marketing is still in its infancy. Talk about a great opportunity!

I can't sell

You know, for most people it's really about fear: *How would I overcome my fear of talking to people?*

I understand how you feel. Many people are uncomfortable with the idea of sales, especially if they have never operated a business. In fact, I felt the same way. May I make a suggestion? Why don't you become a customer? Give the products a try. Become familiar with them. See if you like them. You know what I found? It's not so hard to recommend something that you believe in. Let's see if that happens for you, too.

YOU JUST WANT SOMETHING FROM ME

It feels to me like you are unsure of my motives: *What is it you are really after?*

Okay, I can understand how you might feel that way. May I be upfront with you? Please know that I say this with a right heart: the truth is that I don't want something from you; quite honestly, you don't have anything that I want.

This is not about me getting something from you. I am never going to get where I want to be by taking things from people or by needing things from people. This is about me giving something to you and others. But, you have to want it. If you don't want it, that's okay. I just ask that you clearly understand my intentions.

Often, the objection is just a smokescreen for a deeper issue. Usually that issue is fear; people don't believe in themselves but they are afraid to admit it. It may also be that they are simply not interested but they don't want to hurt your feelings. If you find yourself addressing one objection after another with the same person, this is a clear indication that there is more to the objection than an unanswered question. It's time for you to move on.

Never let handling objections resort to gamesmanship. This is not about turning a "No" into a "Yes." You may win the game, but you lose in the end. Nothing is gained by outsmarting or outmaneuvering another person. The whole point of addressing objections is to help the other person make an informed decision. That decision may be "Yes" or it may be "No." Let their decision be their decision.

Quick Review: Prospecting

1) Don't assume that everyone you talk to is a prospect. Not everyone is looking for what you have.
2) Prospecting is a sorting process. You are simply separating the "Yes" from the "No."
3) When people tell you "No," they are not rejecting *you*. Don't take it personally.
4) Qualify your prospects; don't spend time with the wrong people.
5) Don't prejudge! Desire is more important than ability.
6) Think of objections as unanswered questions.

Exercise

1) Describe an instance where you invested time and energy with someone who was not right for the business. What was the result of that relationship? Did they join the business? If so, how did they do? What did you learn from that experience?

2) You are talking to a prospect who says your products or services are expensive. He also says that he can't sell. Role-play this scenario with your upline or another networker. How should you respond to his objections?

EIGHT

Downline-Upline Relationships

As a network marketer, you are connected to people all around you. You are a downline with upline supporting you and at the same time you are an upline supporting those below you. You have to function as both at the same time.

In this chapter, we will explain how upline and downline work together, and what you should do in both roles. As you read the material, consider it from both sides. With each topic, ask yourself: What is expected of me as a downline in this situation? What is expected of me as an upline? (If you are new to the business, you may not have a downline quite yet. However, you should consider the material as if you already do.)

One final point before we move on: your job as a downline is to be teachable; your job as an upline is to be duplicatable. It's really that simple. You need to lead and inspire, yet be willing to take instruction. You need to heed the teaching and wisdom of your upline and model these for your downline. Think of yourself as a conduit, a channel through which knowledge and wisdom are received and flow freely downstream to others.

Developing Trust

In Chapter 3, we discussed how the relationship capital we bring to our business is our most precious asset. Naturally, we are very protective of our relationships because we have so much invested in them. It follows, then, that trust is a huge consideration as we go about our business.

If you are going to be successful in network marketing, you will have to be trustworthy. You will need to develop trust with your prospects, trust with your downline and trust with your upline.

Your network marketing business is much like the dating process that leads to marriage. You meet someone who shows you an opportunity, but in this case the proposition is not one of marriage; it is a business. You like this person and like what the opportunity has to offer. The next step is for you to meet the parents or in this case your sponsor's upline. In time, you may meet some other people who have already joined the business, the equivalent of your siblings and extended family.

During this "courtship," you develop an impression of your potential sponsor and any upline you meet. You see how they look, what they say, how they act, how they treat other people. You get a pretty good idea of their values and whether or not those values align with yours.

You also learn about the company, its products and services and its compensation plan. You hear testimonials from people who are using the products and from people who are building a business. They "testify" to the integrity of the company, the effectiveness of the products and the validity of the opportunity.

You are evaluating everything you see and hear. Thoughts and questions flow through your mind:

This business looks good but can it really be true?

Will other people buy this?

OK, so maybe they can do it but I'm not sure I can.

Can I trust these people with my future?

Can I trust them with my friends and family?

These are all things that need to be worked out to your satisfaction before you feel comfortable "joining the family," so to speak, and introducing the opportunity to others.

Trust Is Built Through Familiarity

We don't give away our heart on a whim and we don't get married after one date. A considerable getting-to-know-you period must come first. Your business is the same way. Your prospect is not really choosing a company or a product; they are choosing a business partner. They are choosing you.

A great way for them to get to know you (and for you to get to know them) is to have a social gathering. Have a cookout or game night at your house and invite your prospects and new downline to bring their families. Have fun, socialize and talk about anything EXCEPT the business. This is a time to become familiar with each other as individuals and families, not as business associates. Do you have any common interests, such as hobbies or civic concerns? What are you each passionate about? What significant experiences in your life have shaped your values? Some of us grew up poor. Some of us had only one parent, or no parents. Some of us lost a loved one to a disease or accident, or have had a severe medical issue of our own. When we meet people who have had experiences similar to ours—good or bad—we tend to form a bond with them.

If your downline are in another part of the country (or in another country) you can do something similar on the phone or the Internet. However, if you need to build the relationship long-distance, you may want to limit the participants to you, one downline networker and one upline support.

Trust Is Built Through Reliability & Accountability

When you say you are going to do something, do you do it? When you say you will be somewhere at a certain time, are you there...at that time? Being reliable is a great way to build trust with your downline, your upline and everyone around you.

For instance, imagine that your new downline has set an appointment to introduce you by phone to a prospect. You agree to be available for the call, but at the designated time she cannot reach you. What does that do to her trust in you? She talked you up to her prospect, who was excited to meet you—and you weren't there. You made her look foolish and may have even caused her to lose business. What do you suppose will happen the next time she needs her upline? She'll probably call someone else, or try to go it alone.

Granted, there will be times when emergencies come up or you are so busy that you forget about your commitment. We're all human; it happens. When you drop the ball, be sure to make proper amends and hold yourself accountable. Your downline may politely say, "Oh, that's okay; it's not a big deal." But, don't let it go at that. "No, it *is* a big deal," you should say. "I didn't follow through and that's a problem. How can I make it up to you?"

There will be times, too, when you simply don't feel like doing one more three-way call or one more appointment, or sharing your story *one more time.* You are doing all of those things to build your own business and now you have several downline, all who need you to do a three-way call, go on an appointment with them or share your story.

It's a Saturday night and you're scheduled to talk with your downline and her prospect and all you want to do is curl up on the sofa and turn on the television. *You are sick and tired of sharing your story!*

This is where you need to be careful that your fatigue doesn't affect your attitude. You need to be excited, engaging and helpful. Your downline is counting on you; they trust you to be on top of your game. For all you know, this is the prospect at the top of their chicken list and they have finally summoned the courage to call her.

Remember, too, that you represent hope to that prospect on the other end of the phone. They don't know you've shared your story a million times. Tell it with the same enthusiasm, passion and compassion that you did the first time you told it. Never forget that you were once where they are now.

When you commit to doing something, do it. Do it in a timely fashion and do it genuinely.

Trust Is Built Through Transparency

Your new downline will bring a lot of excitement and hope to their business, but also a fair amount of uncertainty, doubt and fear. They will naturally look up to you, particularly if you have been in the business for a while. They may assume that the business is easy for you, that you never had any of the doubts or fears that they do. (We all look good from a distance, don't we?)

Tell them that everyone in this business experiences those things, including you. Share a story about the first time you gave a public presentation to a room full of people and you were so nervous you were certain you were going to pass out. Maybe you said something inadvertently that was really funny or had a marketing idea that went horribly wrong.

Some of your best teaching will come through sharing the mistakes you have made. "We impress people with our success," says leadership expert John Maxwell. "We impact them with our failures."[1]

Understand that we are not suggesting you portray yourself as a bumbling fool or a shrinking violet who just happened to build a business despite herself. After all, you need to have their respect if you are going to lead them. What we are saying is that it's helpful to be transparent, to be a bit vulnerable. When we do this, people identify with us more—*Wow, she really* is *human*—and will feel secure coming to us with their hopes and their fears. That gives us the opportunity to act as the leader we are.

TRUST IS BUILT THROUGH RESPECT

When we treat everyone the same, regardless of their education, ability, wealth, experience and social status, we build trust. The person who starts his or her business today deserves the same respect as the multi-millionaires who have thousands of people in their group.

This includes the way we refer to the people in our organization. When introducing them, never say, "I'd like you to meet my new downline." They are not *yours*. We are all independent, right? None of us works for anyone. Instead, say something like, "I'd like you to meet Stella. She just started her business!" Imagine the bond you will build with Stella when you acknowledge her in that manner instead of making it sound like she is a subordinate.

Remember that respect is a given; it is *dis*respect that is earned.

TRUST IN ACTION

We've said it before, but it's worth repeating: the sooner you can help your downline get their business started, the better. They should take action within 48 hours. Sitting down with them to review their list of contacts is a great way to help them do that and at the same time build their faith in you.

If they have not yet made a list, you can help them write it out. Have them write the first 10 people that come to mind. Almost everyone will start their list with the people they are closest to and are most comfortable approaching. Let's suppose you are working with Sharon, who just joined your group. The two of you are looking at the first several names on her list. The conversation might go something like this:

You: *Tell me about Linda, the first person on your list here. What made you think of her?*

Sharon: *That's my sister. We're very close. I put her first because, well, quite honestly, I think she would be supportive of me. I don't think she would tell me I shouldn't be doing one of those "home-based business things." Whenever either of us gets excited about something, we always call each other first. Is that an okay reason?*

You: *Absolutely. It's a great reason! Sharon, we all start this business from a place of uneasiness. In the beginning, I had no idea what I was doing. I worried a lot about what people would think of me. I knew in my heart that I had my hands on something fantastic, but we all know that other people don't always see it that way. You obviously know Linda quite well. What does she want out of life? Why would this business be attractive to her?*

Sharon: *Well, we talk a lot about needing more money for things like the kids' tuition and our retirement. We both have a good household income, but like Linda was just saying the other day, we're only about 15 years from retirement age and we have nearly nothing saved.*

You: *So, what do you think you would say to her?*

Sharon: *I don't know. That's the hardest part, I think, trying to figure out how to say everything the right way. What would you say to her?*

You: *I would just share my heart. Don't worry about saying it perfectly. You might tell her exactly what you just told me. "Linda: Hi, it's me. Hey, you know how when we get excited about something we always call each other first? Well, I found something. Weren't we just talking the other day*

about not having enough put away for retirement? Well, I've got it. I found the answer! You have got to see this!"
Sharon: *Okay, okay, yes, I like that. I know I could do that.*

During this conversation, you have established trust with Sharon in multiple ways:
1) You spent time with her. You invested *your* time in *her* future;
2) You validated her fears about what to say to her prospects and also about what other people might think and say.
3) You assured her by acknowledging that you had similar fears.
4) You were transparent.

Your conversation continues:
You: *How about the next person on your list: Joel?*
Sharon: *Joel and I share an office. He's always talking about how he doesn't like his job. He's been thinking of quitting for a long time. He has said many times he doesn't know what to do with his life.*
You: *And, how might you approach Joel?*
Sharon: *Repeat what he has told me, just like I did with Linda, and then tell him why I'm excited?*
You: *You got it! Let's hear you say it.*
Sharon: *Okay, here goes: "Joel, you know how you're always talking about needing to do something different, how you're not happy here? Well, I just learned about something you need to take a look at. The people I have met are making money, they're helping other people and they absolutely love what they are doing."*
You: *Great! Excellent!*

In addition to establishing trust with Sharon:
1) you encouraged her; and
2) in both instances, you gave her suggestions, not dictates.

You will have downline who are hesitant to give you access to their list of contacts. Remember, we all have a lot invested in our relationship capital and we're naturally very protective of it. Your downline may worry that you will come on too strong, that you will be pushy or offensive in some way. They are afraid of being embarrassed or that you will damage their relationships.

Countless friendships have been spoiled—who knows how many permanently?—because of irresponsible upline trying to strong arm their downline's prospects. Imagine the damage we do when we are aggressive, pompous and selfish. We demonstrate that what we want is more important than anything else and we tarnish the entire industry.

More discussion with Sharon:

You: *Okay, now, remember that when you contact people, your goal is to introduce them to me and your other upline. You should get us involved right away.*

    Sharon: *Uhm...uh...I guess so...I mean, I can try...*

You: *Sharon, you sound a bit hesitant. Are you uncomfortable with the thought of me talking to the people on your list?*

    Sharon: *Well, now that you mention it, yes, I am. I mean, I've known a lot of these people a long time and I think it would just be better if I talked to them. I already know them...*

You: *And, you are worried that I or someone else in your upline will say something to upset them, that we will be pushy or try to talk them into something against their will. Something like that?*

    Sharon: *(laughing nervously) Yep, that pretty much sums it up!*

You: *Well, Sharon, first of all thank you for being honest. It's important that we're always upfront with each other. Second, I understand what you are saying. None of us wants to alienate a friend or family member. Do you know who is great at sorting these things out? Gwen! Do you remember meeting her?*

    Sharon: *Yes, yes, I do.*

You: *Okay, I'm going to call her. I know she'll have some great insights on this.*

You call Gwen and bring her into the conversation. You let Sharon share her concerns with Gwen while you remain quiet. You do not offer any additional input, but instead give Gwen the opportunity to form a deeper relationship with Sharon. Gwen validates Sharon's fears, just as you did. Gwen suggests that they do a role-play, with Gwen playing herself and Sharon playing the part of one of the people on her list. Gwen models for Sharon how she would talk to Sharon's prospect.

Sharon feels much better after this and is now comfortable connecting both you and Gwen to the people on her list.

Let's pause a moment one more time to review your exchange with Sharon. When she acknowledged her hesitancy to give you access to her prospects, you handled it expertly:

1) you once again validated her concerns; you didn't laugh it off or otherwise dismiss it;

2) you reassured her, genuinely, that you will never do anything to embarrass her or put her relationships at risk;

3) you brought in another upline member, Gwen, so she could build trust with Sharon as well;

4) you modeled several things for Sharon that she can duplicate through her downline:

- invest time in others;
- validate fears;
- acknowledge your own struggles;
- encourage others;
- give suggestions, not orders;
- bring in upline to answer questions.

Communicate And Confide

Relationships cannot remain in a healthy state without good communication. This includes the relationships in your business. Be honest and forthright about your fears; confide in the support team above you. They have walked the battlefields of this business and will be a great comfort to you.

If your upline does something to upset you, bring it to their attention, respectfully. Expect that they will do the same when they are offended by something that *you* say or do. Work out any differences before they fester and infect your business.

Tell your upline about your Dream; they should be encouraging you to do so anyway. Many network marketers never share their WHY. It could be that they haven't yet figured it out, but often the reason is that they are afraid to tell anyone. Stating their WHY makes it real, and once it's real it is something they can fail at. If there is a chance they can fail, many people would rather not try at all.

They may also be afraid that their W<small>HY</small> won't meet their upline's expectations, that it isn't big enough. Maybe all they want is to pay for their children's college education. If they have an upline whose W<small>HY</small> is to have total time and financial freedom—*it doesn't get any bigger than that!*—they may worry that the same is expected of them.

Don't worry about the expectations of others. If your upline is truly in this business to help you and not just themselves, it won't matter *what* your W<small>HY</small> is; they'll help you accomplish it. But, they are not mind-readers. You have to tell them what you want.

As an upline, don't expect more out of your downline than they are willing to give. Let them decide for themselves how successful they will be. If your downline stay in this business because they are afraid to disappoint you, they will become frustrated and eventually resentful of you. If you sense this is happening, take the initiative and talk to them. Remind them that they are in this for themselves, not for you. Reassure them that your respect for them is not determined by the size of their business.

All of the things we have been talking about in this chapter—trust, hope, fear, values—are issues of the heart; they strike at our very core. Work to develop a relationship with your upline and downline where you can be totally transparent with each other. It will do wonders for your business, but also for your personal development. As one network marketer often says, "My sponsor knows me down to my underwear."

Be Teachable

As we mentioned before, your No. 1 job as a downline is to be teachable. You need to listen, receive wisdom, and not try to do this business by yourself. Proverbs instructs us to have a proper attitude: "To learn, you must want to be taught."[2]

Perhaps you are inclined to tell your upline, "Thanks, but I can do this myself. I don't need to take you along." You decide to develop your goals without their input, talk to your prospects on your own, ignore the team training and teach your downline yourself. After all, you are smart, educated and experienced and this can't really be that hard, can it?

Many network marketers believe they don't need to learn anything, or that their upline aren't smart enough to teach them. They are what we refer to as a Frank Sinatra (as in "I did it *my* way.") If that is how you intend to operate your business, we have a message for you: you will likely fail.

We're sorry if that sounds harsh, but it's the truth. You will never build a network marketing business that is solid and sustainable if you try to do it all on your own. Have you considered that the industry has been around for some 70 years and if there is a better way to do things, someone would have discovered it by now?

(Now, before you go getting your knickers in a knot wanting to argue that the Internet has changed the rules and it's a completely new game, let us acknowledge that the worldwide web *is* important and yes, we *are* proponents of using it to build your business. We will address that later.)

The point here is that many people in this business who came before you also tried to reinvent the wheel. Chances are, what you are doing (or thinking of doing) is not new. Somewhere in your upline is someone who can tell you all about the landmines he or she stepped on while running the battlefield alone. They can testify that if they would have listened to their upline—these are the seasoned soldiers who know where the mines are—they could have avoided blowing themselves up. You should listen, too.

Working With The Unteachable

So, as the sponsor to a Frank Sinatra (or Frannie, as the case may be) what do you do? First, understand that you can't *make* Frank or Frannie do *anything*. We're all independent. You can't demand to be involved in their business.

They are typically a Type A personality, a choleric. They may be a go-getter but are also the hardest to work with. They have a high degree of self-confidence, but also a sizeable ego. They are always making statements instead of asking questions. If they can't order people around, they are lost. They're just not good at building relationships.

The bottom line is that you pretty much have to let them do what they are determined to do. However, you should attempt to explain to them the danger in it. Given the personality type, you may want to frame your conversation with, "May I make a suggestion?" You have to get their okay on it. You can't just say, "This is what you're doing wrong."

You can't have control issues yourself; don't let *your* ego get in the way. Remember, Frank and Frannie think they know more than you do. So, you tell them, "This is what we have found works. Other people have tried what you're doing but from experience we can tell you that it doesn't work."

Explain to them that they are not duplicatable. Few, if any, of the people they sponsor will have the same level of skill and experience that they have. If the people they bring in see their sponsor doing everything on his or her own, they will naturally conclude that they have to do the same. And, that will discourage them. This does not bode well for Frank's or Frannie's business.

Second, explain to them that their workload will dramatically increase. Without their upline involved, their downline will have only one place to turn for help. Do they really want to be depended upon for *everything*?

Third, point out some of the mistakes they will likely make, for instance saying the wrong things, failing to do follow-up, not listening to people's needs. Demonstrate that you have the knowledge and experience to help them avoid derailing their own business.

Assure them that they have the right to continue to do it their way, but also ask them: "Will you promise me one thing?" Wait for a response. *Yeah, okay.* "If, in the first 30 days you discover it's not working for you, understand that the door is open for you to come back and talk about how we can help you be successful. Can we have that understanding between us?" *Sure.*

Let them go out and do their thing. If they come back, wanting help, welcome them with open arms and go to work. If they don't come back, they were never going to build it anyway. You haven't wasted any more time with them and the relationship hasn't ended negatively.

When they quit and their friends ask, "So, that *thing* you were doing, how's it going?" they can say, "Oh, it wasn't what they said it was; it doesn't work" or they can say, "The business works; I just didn't do it properly." If they're honest, they will say the latter.

They Must Want It For Themselves

Have you ever sponsored someone into the business only to wait for them to get started, and wait...and wait...and wait? If you haven't, well, just give it time. Eventually, you will sponsor the guy or gal who just sits at the starting gate forever. In fact, you will sponsor many such people.

They will say things like:

"I'm going to have my list ready real soon."

"I'm going to be setting appointments in a few days."

"I'm going to have my goals written in no time."

"I'm going to have people in my business before you know it!"

Every organization has an "Ima Gonna." *I'm a gonna do this* and *I'm a gonna do that.* These are the people who are always "going to do" something but never actually do *anything!* Don't listen to what people say; watch their feet. The truth is in their actions, not their words.

The best thing you can do for you and for Ima is to go work with someone else. Find your runners and run with them. Ima may be your best friend and a very, very sweet person. But, you cannot want this business for her. She has to want it for herself.

Leading vs. Managing

You may come to this business with significant management experience or sales and marketing experience. Perhaps you have owned a business. You might have a marketing degree, even an MBA. You were promoted through the ranks of your company to a high-level management position. You have won numerous industry awards.

If that describes you, congratulations! (We mean that sincerely.) You obviously have talent and have worked hard for your success. However, while many of your skills and experiences are transferrable to this business, the rules you have been playing by in the corporate marketplace are not.

In the corporate world, people are motivated mostly by fear. If they don't get their work done, they risk being disciplined, having their pay docked or worse, being fired. The job of their supervisor or manager is to make sure they do what they are instructed to do.

As a network marketer, you cannot manage people; nor should you try. You need to *lead* them. Network marketers don't need to be told what to do; they need to be *shown* what to do. You are in a completely new game, and you cannot bring old rules to a new game.

Managing is making sure people stay on the job until their work is done (and done right); leading is inspiring people and creating a vision. Managing is calculating and rational; leading is intuitive and empathetic. Managing is about how we do things; leading is about *why* we do things.

Managing says, "You will build my Dream" while leading says, "Come with me; let's build our Dream together."

It's not surprising that certain network marketers who are used to telling people what to do often struggle to grasp the idea of leadership. They've never had to work with people who are essentially "volunteering" to be led and not mandated to report to them. In the corporate world, managers can use the authority of their position to keep their underlings in line. However, while employees have to respect the manager's position of authority, they do not have to respect *him*. They only do what they are told because they must.

He might be very good at his job, but he may also be hiding behind that authority. Network marketing, on the other hand, is a real window into our level of personal development. It will expose all of our shortcomings: lack of self-confidence; lack of people skills; excessive ego; control issues; lack of patience. The reason many people in this business aren't teachable is that they don't want their shortcomings exposed for the whole world to see.

But, when we are willing to admit we're not perfect, stretch ourselves beyond our comfort zone and invest in others for their sake and not only ours, we will inspire people. They in turn will inspire others. The example we set also creates a high degree of loyalty, to the point that our downline attribute much of *their* personal development to our mentoring.

Be a leader, not a manager. And, if you really want to know which you are, look behind you. If people are following you, you are a leader. If no one is there, perhaps you are just out for a stroll.

Coax Them Out Of The Nest

Encourage your new downline to do the presentation at an open meeting as soon as they have a basic grasp of the material. Like baby birds afraid to leave the nest, they may resist getting up in front of a crowd, preferring to wait until they think they are ready. Nonetheless, you should try to get them to fly quickly, for several reasons:

1) *They develop more rapidly.* We cannot grow without doing things that are uncomfortable. Many people absolutely dread public speaking; they would rather face tooth extraction. Being pushed out of the nest forces them to face their fears, and in almost every instance they do much better than they thought they could. It is a boost to their self-confidence and a real shot in the arm for their business.

2) *They are enthusiastic.* New downline have a lot of excitement, and excitement is critical to the success of a meeting. It's not so much what is said, but *how* it is said. Enthusiasm is infectious!

3) *They keep it real.* When new people do the presentation, they frequently make mistakes. They may garble the information on the slides and mispronounce words. Often, it is quite apparent that they are nervous. Some people would think this is unprofessional, that it makes your business look second-rate. But, to the prospects seated in the audience, it is actually encouraging. It shows them that you don't have to be perfect. Keep in mind that most of them think they could never stand up there like that brand new person is doing right now. You want to show them that you don't have to master the business before you *do* the business.

Be careful, however, not to let undeserving people do a public presentation. Being excited isn't enough. They have to be doing the right things and they have to be teachable. Don't reward bad behaviors and habits with additional opportunity and responsibility.

Don't Add The "S"

When we have a new downline networker (or even an excited prospect), we have a tendency toward "mothering" her. Like a momma duck looking after her brood, we instinctively want to nurture and protect her Dream. We have an ongoing checklist running in our heads: *Have I told her about this? Have I told her about that? Have I introduced her to this person? Have I introduced her to that person? She mentioned her friend, Marie; has she called her to set an appointment? She needs to get moving. Oh, yes, I just remembered another thing—I had better call her right now.*

While it is natural and appropriate to look after those who join the business, we need to keep our contact at an appropriate level. Don't call or email people every time you think of something they need to know. You will overwhelm them. You also run the risk of looking domineering; or worse, needy.

Instead, schedule a time to talk about several things at once. Be organized and purposeful, not impulsive. They have a life outside of this business and so do you! Don't let your mothering become *smothering.* The difference between the two is just one letter, but the results are miles apart. Don't sit on your chicks. Don't add the "S"!

Do It With Them, Not For Them

We also need to be careful not to enable our downline. In our desire to be helpful, we might say, "I'll make that call for you," or "I can do follow-up with that prospect if you'd like." We might also think to ourselves, *It will take too long to teach them this stuff; it's faster and easier if I just do it myself.*

We may honestly believe we are helping our downline, but the truth is that we are hindering them. Think about this in terms of parenting. One of the biggest mistakes we can make is to fail to teach our children how to be independent, which means they are dependent on us forever. Once our kids reach a certain age, we shouldn't be checking their homework assignments, laying out their clothes and waking them up in the morning for school. These are things that they are old enough to handle themselves. We may feel a parental urge to continue to do these things, but that is actually a disservice to our children. They will never learn to live on their own.

By making the calls our downline don't want to make, we enable their fears and stifle their personal growth. By doing *anything* for them that they should be doing themselves, we inhibit their learning and foster laziness. The next time they have a prospecting call to make or follow-up to do, they may very well expect us to do it for them. It becomes a learned behavior.

The same goes for answering their questions. When someone asks us a question, what do we naturally do? *We answer the question.* We do it routinely. It's normal and it's the polite thing to do. But, we need to be careful not to answer *every* question or solve *every* problem our downline bring to us. To duplicate yourself, you must avoid being the Answer Man or the Answer Woman.

The power of this business is residual income, right? Remember, that's the money you make long after you stop working the business. That's what gives you the freedom to stop working it if you so choose. Well, how are you ever going to step back and enjoy any amount of freedom if you're the one who knows everything? You *have* to stick around; you're indispensable!

When you always supply the answer, you *become* the answer. *I'll just call my upline. He always knows what to say. I'm sure he's already worked out the answer.* They think you're smart and wise, which is true (and good for your ego), but the problem is that they don't think they could ever be as good as you. Besides, they'll never have to worry about it because you're always there.

When someone says, "You are so wonderful; you always have the answer," that's the time to get worried. It's a sure sign you are not duplicatable. There are a lot of people in this industry who make it all about them and everybody knows their name. They may have a sizeable income, but they also have a lot of turnover in their business because people can't duplicate what is being modeled for them. As a result, the non-duplicatable networker has to work very hard to maintain his income. If he ever slows down, his business will fall apart on him.

We are not saying you should *never* answer your downline's questions. When someone is new and learning the business, you have to help them with certain things: writing invoices; placing orders; calculating volume, for example.

However, many of their questions should be answered (and many of their issues resolved) through their own personal development program and through The System, which we will discuss next.

Remember, everything in this business duplicates; they will do what *you* do. If you teach them to let their upline do everything for them, they will teach the same to their downline. Not only will it stunt their personal growth, it will stunt their business.

Help them find the answer but don't *be* the answer. Do it with them, not *for* them.

Model, don't coddle.

You Are Not Responsible For Their Success

When we sponsor someone into the business, we're just as excited for them as they are for themselves, perhaps more. We may even feel *responsible* for their success. We may come to believe that because we showed them the opportunity, encouraged them to dream again and gave them hope, we have to make this business work for them. We cannot let them down; it's up to us.

We may even blame ourselves when things go wrong. *Oh, no! What am I going to do? Lisa was so excited; she had such high expectations. And, now she's miserable and going to quit. Why did I encourage her to join this business? I wish I had never even talked to her about it. It was all a big mistake. What if she won't forgive me?*

If you are carrying this burden, we are giving you permission, right here and now, to put it down. It is not yours to carry; it never was. You are not responsible for their success and you should not beat yourself up when people quit. They, like you and everyone else in this business, are independent and responsible for their own success.

As long as you have not told them this is easy, guaranteed how much money they will make, told them they were going to be great or made other promises, you have no reason to feel responsible.

Tell people in the beginning what it takes to build this business. Be genuine and forthcoming and your conscience will remain clear.

Reach Down And Lift Up

The corporate world has a rigid reporting structure. The line staff report to their supervisors, the supervisors report to managers, who report to vice-presidents who report to the president. Rarely, if ever, does anyone communicate with someone who is not directly above or below them. This is done deliberately for the sake of order and efficiency.

However, this is one of many corporate rules that do not apply to your business. There will be times when you need to reach down and around downline who are immediately below you, so that you can work directly with leaders who are deeper within your organization.

Let's say that Monica, who is on your third level, is generating a lot of activity. You recognize that the two people in between you and her, Eduardo and Gabriela, are not ready to help her. They are still developing their leadership skills, or they are not teachable or perhaps they are simply not actively building their business. Perhaps Monica and you have similar personalities and you just "click." She is more comfortable working with you than she is with either of them. There is nothing wrong with that.

Eduardo and Gabriela have already introduced you to Monica. If they haven't, let them know that you will be contacting Monica and offering to help her and mentor her.

Be careful to protect your relationship with Eduardo and Gabriela. It should never be a surprise to them that you are working closely with one of their downline. Don't blindside them. Remember, trust is critical and to have trust you must have good communication.

If Eduardo and Gabriela don't respect you and don't trust the way you do the business, then you need to address *that* issue first. They may instinctively try to "protect" Monica from you. *What are you doing, messing with one of my people? How dare you do that without my permission?!*

If, however, you have a healthy relationship with them (and if they are smart), they will welcome your desire to work directly with Monica. After all, the larger Monica's business grows, the more they benefit.

While there is absolutely nothing ethically wrong with you reaching down to Monica, don't disregard her upline's feelings. Remember, were it not for them, Monica would not be in this business and you would not have the opportunity to work with her.

If you maintain a healthy relationship with Eduardo and Gabriela, you may see some other unexpected (but wonderful) results. As Monica grows into a leader and produces momentum in her business, this will create income for Eduardo and Gabriela. That may cause them to be more confident in themselves and in turn start talking to more prospects. It might also create a sense of urgency in them. *Hey, look at what Monica is doing. I had better get going!*

Be aware of the leaders in your organization and reach out to them wherever they are. But, at all times be respectful of your downline who are in between. Encourage them and let them know when you are reaching down and around.

Lead The Pack

You are the one at the front of your organization. You are the "lead dog." And, as the lead dog you determine how fast your organization will move. In other words, the speed of the leader is the speed of the pack. If the leader is running, those in the pack who want to run will have someone to follow. However, if the leader doesn't move then they probably won't either.

You need to understand that your downline are looking to you and at you. They are looking *to* you to provide guidance and wisdom and *at* you to see if you are practicing what you preach. If they see you talking to new people, sponsoring and moving your business ahead, those who want to build a business will do the same.

When you sponsor new people and help them get started, you are modeling for your downline how the business works and that it *does* work. You are also creating a sense of urgency. They can see that you are not sitting back waiting for them to get going. You are looking for more leaders. You aren't a dog who *talks* about running; you *do* it.

If your new downline is the only one you're working with, at some point he is going to say, "Well, this guy is not that good. I'm all he's got going." But, if he sees you generating activity, bringing guests, sponsoring and giving time to other downline, that changes the dynamic. He knows that if he wants your help, he is going to have to chase you.

For people who are somewhat "retired" from the business, this is not necessarily applicable. They have developed other leaders beneath them who are now leading their own packs and their intimate involvement isn't really needed. At some point, everyone earns the right to step back and enjoy the lifestyle they have worked so hard to build.

However, to get to that place you need to lead the pack for a long time. Continue to set the example by talking to new people. Remember that leadership is about modeling—not telling people what to do, but *showing* them what to do.

Don't expect your downline to do what you are unwilling to do yourself. Set the pace and the pack will follow.

Give Without Guarantee

As an upline in this business, you must make considerable investment in other people with no guarantee of anything in return. This is another major departure from the corporate business model.

In the corporate world, return on investment (ROI) is the measuring stick for most business decisions. When a company makes a human resources investment (hiring and paying someone), the company expects a return on that investment. If an employee is lazy, uncooperative, incompetent, misses work frequently or is otherwise counterproductive, he is fired.

In network marketing, everyone is independent and therefore no one works under the fear of being fired. That is good because positive motivation (having a Dream) replaces negative motivation (the fear of being fired). However, it also presents a certain reality for you: you must give of yourself with no guarantee of getting anything back.

One of the major criticisms of network marketing is that people make money off the people below them. (By the way, have you noticed how this concept is praised in the corporate marketplace yet decried as unethical in network marketing?) The truth is that the people who are just getting into the business—these are the so called "victims" of network marketing—are the ones who assume the least risk. They make a relatively modest monetary investment, which often comes with a money-back guarantee.

Their sponsor and upline, however, assume *significant* risk. They teach, train and mentor their downline with no guarantee of even a penny of return on that investment. Many seasoned network marketers have the skills, experience and wisdom to earn huge incomes as consultants in the corporate marketplace. Yet, they give all of that away for free to their downline.

Understand that you will have to make the same non-guaranteed investment, time after time after time. Most of the people you sponsor will not build a business despite your best efforts at helping them. *Que sera, sera;* that's just the way it is. The good news is that you will also develop leaders whose efforts will repay you handsomely and more than make up for the rest.

Invest Your Time Wisely

Your downline should not have *carte blanche* access to you; they must earn it. Your time is a capital investment and you need to invest it wisely. You have no obligation to invest in the wrong people. Make sure that you are giving your time only to downline who deserve it. On the surface that may sound harsh, but it is sound business practice. You need to invest in people who are hungry, teachable and taking action. You can't devote your business energies to Frank Sinatra and Ima Gunna.

You will have many good-hearted, well-meaning people in your downline who become dear friends but are never going to build a business. Give them your love and friendship, but also realize that when you have blocked out time in your day to work on your business, you cannot give that time to a thirty-minute chat about what's going on in their lives. Jealously guard the time you set aside for your business.

Quick Review: Downline-Upline Relationships

1) Mutual trust and respect are essential to building a solid business.
2) Communicate. Be clear with your upline about what you want from this business.
3) Be teachable. Be willing to take instruction.
4) As an upline, you cannot help those who are not teachable.
5) You cannot want this business for your downline; they must want it for themselves.
6) Lead. Don't manage.
7) Don't add the "S." Don't sit on your chicks.
8) Do the business *with* your downline, not *for* them.
9) You are not responsible for their success; they are.
10) You will have to reach down and around to find your leaders.
11) The speed of the leader is the speed of the pack. Don't expect your downline to do things that you won't do.
12) You must invest in people with no guarantee of anything in return.
13) Invest your time only in those who deserve it.

Exercise

1) Write down examples of how you have built trust with your downline, or how your upline has built trust with you. If you have not yet started a business, write down how you would build trust with the people you sponsor.

2) Role play with your upline. You play the part of yourself and your upline plays the part of Sharon, whom you have just sponsored. Sharon is reluctant to give you access to the people on her list of contacts. She would prefer that you not meet them until she has already sponsored them into the business. Explain to her why it's important to her success to have her upline involved right from the start.

NINE

Duplication Through The System

At the turn of the 20th century, automobiles were the plaything of the rich. They were expensive and complicated. But, Henry Ford had a vision: he would build an automobile that was simple to operate and that everyone could afford.

In 1913, Ford incorporated the "assembly line" system into the production of his vehicles. It was a stroke of genius that revolutionized the industry. For the first time, a car could be assembled quickly and cost-effectively, and for the first time middle-income Americans could afford to own one. By 1926, the Ford Motor Company had sold 15 million of its Model T cars.

Like Ford, any organization that has sustained value, that is successful for long periods of time, has a "System." The System serves to standardize the organization's activities, making those activities understandable and duplicatable and thereby making the organization run more smoothly and more efficiently. The System teaches new people how to use their current skills and how to develop new ones that will contribute to the advancement of themselves and the organization. The System eliminates confusion, saves time, perfects processes, fosters cohesiveness and produces momentum and growth, within both the organization and the individual.

Schools have systems consisting of a particular curriculum, scheduled class times, standardized tests, and advancement from one grade to the next, culminating with graduation.

A military is perhaps the best example of the effective use of a system. Regimented procedures are critical; the lives of soldiers and the sovereignty of nations are at stake.

How A System Works

Your network marketing business should also have a system. Chances are your group or company already has a well-established one in place. However, if you are part of a start-up company, you may find yourself helping establish The System.

Systems vary from company to company and often among groups within the same company. The basic components generally consist of a combination of the following:

1) Your upline;
2) Open meetings;
3) Business training;
4) Business conferences;
5) Webinars;
6) Three-way calls;
7) Conference calls;
8) Personal development program; and
9) Other marketing tools, such as advertising.

The System is the collective efforts, wisdom and experiences of people who through trial and error have become successful in the business. They have perfected the process. They have walked the walk, blazed the trail, stepped on the land mines and the cow pies and lived to tell about it.

The System exists for your benefit; it is there for you to use. In the next several paragraphs we will outline the various ways The System can help you. Take advantage of The System and your business has the potential to blow the doors off your Dream. Disregard it and you will be in deep water without a lifeline.

Borrow Strength

A majority of the people who come into this business have no sales or marketing experience and no business background of any kind. They doubt their abilities, they're often overwhelmed and in many cases are downright scared. It's all they can do just to sponsor someone; just doing *that much* is more than they thought they could ever do. *On top of that, you want me to mentor someone? Holy smokes! How am I going to do THAT?!*

In the beginning, you won't have all of the knowledge, experience and confidence that you will eventually need. But, the beauty of The System is that you don't have to! You can borrow strength from your upline. They will help you do presentations, assist you with follow-up and help you address your prospect's objections. Your upline will work with the people you bring in, just as they are working with you. They will mentor them at the same time they are mentoring you.

In time, you will develop skills and wisdom to lend to your downline. Until then, borrow from your upline.

BUILD IT IMMEDIATELY

The System gives you the chance to build your business straight away. You don't have to graduate from school, complete an apprenticeship or pass a test. You don't really have to know much of anything. If you can bring people to The System and plug them in, you can make money now. In this business, you hear people say time and time again, "I made 500 dollars my first month and to this day I don't know how I did it," or "I had no idea how to do this business in the beginning, but I made 2,000 dollars in my first six weeks." These are the people who are excited, who take action right away and simply use The System.

The System is your track to run on. All you have to do is lace up your sneakers and go!

SAVE TIME

We are all busy. We were busy before we started our business and we're even busier now. Wouldn't you welcome something that would help you build your business while also saving you time? Well, The System does that.

Suppose you have just finished an appointment with a prospect. Before you leave, you hand him a CD. It is an audio recording of a presentation given by one of the top networkers in your company. The CD underscores all of the things you were just sharing with your prospect, such as having a Dream and building residual income. He listens to the CD in his car or at another convenient time and it provides follow-up without you having to be there.

You can also have the prospect look at an on-line presentation or have new networkers view an online training. Because you do not have to be present when they use these business tools, you again save time while moving your business forward.

You can bring five people to one open meeting instead of having to do five individual appointments. You can host a conference call for all of your new downline and speak to them as a group instead of making dozens of individual telephone calls. This works well when you have new people from all over the country (or all over the world).

Take advantage of the time-saving opportunities that The System makes available, but keep in mind that you still have to allow for plenty of one-on-one time with your prospects and downline. Remember that saving time is not your top priority; people are.

CONVENIENCE

Isn't the electrical system in your home great? There are outlets throughout the house, several to a room, sometimes two or more on one wall. All you have to do is walk over and plug in your computer, lamp, television or whatever needs power. How convenient!

Imagine, instead, that every time you bought something that needed electrical power, you would have to design and build a power source for it. How *inconvenient* would that be?

The System in your business is just like the electrical system in your home; all you have to do is find an outlet and plug people into it. You have several outlets to choose from: the open meeting, your upline, conference calls and so on. Each element of The System is a power outlet with easy access.

You bring people, plug them in and The System provides the power! And, if your prospect or downline lives far away from you, you can plug them in remotely via the telephone, Internet and open meetings that are in their area.

CONSISTENCY

Another great feature of an electrical system is that the power is consistent. No matter where you plug in your device, you will get a standard power output. Similarly, you know that your prospects will get a consistent opportunity presentation, consistent training and consistent mentoring from your upline.

Furthermore, The System doesn't care what your downline networker's background is, how much experience she has, or how polished her leadership skills are. The System develops and respects everyone equally, regardless of their level of personal development.

MAXIMIZE MOMENTUM

When you have a flurry of activity, many people joining in a short period of time, this will create momentum in your business. Momentum builds in waves, and when the wave comes you need to ride it! And, you use The System to maximize the ride.

If you were to sponsor three people in a relatively short amount of time and each of them sponsored three as quickly as you did, that would be 12 new people in your organization who need follow-up, who are setting appointments, acquiring customers and developing business goals. Even if you are Superman, there is no way you can keep up with the needs of 12 new people in your business. You might be able to help two or three (perhaps even four) but the rest would have to wait.

While they waited, they would lose excitement and all of the naysayers would have an easier time trying to kill their Dream. Your business would lose momentum.

Once again, you just plug the new people into The System. And guess what? While it's possible to overload yourself, you cannot overload The System. *You* might blow a fuse, but The System won't. It just expands as necessary.

No one is going to say, "Sorry, you are bringing way too many people to the open meetings. We can't let you do that anymore." Your upline is not going to say, "Hey, wait a minute. That's just way too many people joining all at once. You need to slow down."

To the contrary, they will rally around you. When there is a buzz created in The System, everybody benefits. So, when you have momentum, use The System to ride the wave. The more you use it the better!

POSITIVE REINFORCEMENT

There will be times when it is hard for you to maintain a positive attitude, when this business frustrates you, when it seems like everybody you meet is just a "No" waiting to happen, when for the umpteenth time you've had a relative laugh at you and tell you that you should just get a better job.

These are the times when you will be so mad, so frustrated, so discouraged…that you just want to quit. And, these are the times that you need The System more than ever. Remember, the world wants nothing better than to keep you where you are, to steal your Dream. This is precisely when you need an injection of positive reinforcement, a safe place to go where people support you and lift you up instead of tearing you down.

Go to an open meeting, get on a conference call or go to your upline for some encouragement. Pull out your favorite motivational CD and listen to it *one more time.* Use The System to remind you that you have a Dream and it is alive and well. Be re-energized. Be inspired!

MODELING

Network marketing is a business of showing, not just telling. The System gives you the opportunity to learn from the top networkers in the business as they model how to effectively do each of the steps: Invitation, Presentation and Follow-up. When you observe a seasoned networker engage a prospect, ask for a decision or give encouragement to someone in her downline, take good notes. By studying your upline, you will perfect your own skills and in turn model them for your downline.

URGENCY

When we see other people bringing guests to an open meeting or being promoted while we remain where we are, it can create a healthy sense of urgency. *Omigosh, Melody just made another level and won a trip. I need to get moving. If she can do it, I can do it!*

We are not suggesting a climate where there is fierce competition, jealousy and gossip. We should always operate in a spirit of lifting each other up. The point here is that seeing another networker advance her business can be a huge motivator for us.

If there was no central System that brought people together for meetings, training and recognition, this impact would be lost. By plugging yourself and your downline into The System, your business will benefit from a healthy sense of urgency.

It's All About Duplication

Have you ever noticed how you tend to do certain things the same way your parents always did them? Most of us fold clothes, make dinner, keep the checkbook, maintain our yard and raise our kids a certain way because that's how our parents did it. We tend to do what is modeled for us.

The same is true of your business. The System exposes your downline to the collective efforts, wisdom and experiences of successful people. The idea is that your downline will duplicate what is being modeled for them. As parents, we want our kids to experience things that make their lives more productive and fulfilling and to avoid the mistakes that make their lives harder. In business, we want the same things. We want to encourage our downline to duplicate what has helped us because it will also help them, and to avoid that which doesn't work.

You must also understand that both good *and bad* duplicate. Just like kids pick up their parents' bad habits, your downline will pick up yours. If you don't return phone calls in a timely manner, they probably won't either. If you don't do follow-up, chances are neither will they. If you don't plug into the System, they probably won't either. Before you do (or neglect to do) anything, give serious thought to how it will duplicate.

WHAT DUPLICATION IS NOT

Unfortunately, some people in network marketing have a wrong-headed idea of duplication. These are the networkers who demand their downline do everything they tell them to do, when they tell them to do it. *Do exactly as I say or I won't help you.* They are intimidators, not mentors.

Duplication does not come from being a drill sergeant or from trying to clone ourselves through our downline. Do not tear people down and try to remake them in your image. If you try to orchestrate every word that comes out of someone's mouth, you steal their identity. If you quash their creativity, you kill their spirit. You will lose your best leaders.

Most people who join network marketing bring with them skills, experience and marketplace ideas from their other careers. Don't ignore that; don't treat new people as if they don't know anything.

Help them identify their strengths and suggest how they can use those strengths in their networking business. Introduce them to personal development resources that will help them grow in areas where they need to grow.

Remember that you must allow people to be themselves, to put *their* stamp on *their* business. You must allow people to have input and give them freedom to make choices.

Ford was an innovative and driven industrialist who did many great things. But he was also unyielding to a fault. He demanded that everything be done his way, often to the peril of his company.

By the mid-1920's, consumers had begun to ask for more sophisticated vehicles. Cheap and practical were no longer most important to them. This was a major market shift, one that Ford refused to acknowledge. When his employees took the initiative to build a prototype Model T with a few modern features, Ford responded by kicking in the windshield and stomping on the roof.

"We got the message," said one employee. "As far as he was concerned, the Model T was God and we were to put away false images."[1]

By 1927, with sales plummeting, Ford abruptly ended production of his Model T. His factory closed for six months while he figured out what to do next.

Don't you make the same mistake. Like a parent, your job is to instruct and model success. But, your downline must be given the opportunity to run their own businesses, even if it means skinning their knees from time to time.

And, like your children, they won't always listen to you. Jesus tells of the prodigal son who rebelled, left home, spent his inheritance foolishly and eventually returned home begging for his father's forgiveness. [2] His father didn't shun him or even punish him. There wasn't one "I told you so!" Instead, he welcomed the son with open arms.

We must have the same attitude. We must, in essence, say to our downline, "I want you to be successful. I will show you what I believe is the best way to do this business, and will help you do it as I have done it. However, I also realize that you have your own identity and you have your own personality. I promise to respect who you are.

"If you want to go build your business in a manner that I do not agree with, I won't try to stop you; I will wish you well. If at any time you discover that it is not working out for you, you are welcome to return and I will greet you with open arms. There will be no correction, no condemnation. We will start anew and I will invest in you with all my heart."

Healthy duplication begins with a right heart. It is training up people in the way that they should go while also respecting their individuality and valuing what they bring to the table.

Invest in people. Develop them. But, let them be who they are.

GET OUT OF THE WAY

As you master the business, you will grow more and more confident. You will become an expert presenter; you will have great poise and your timing will be perfect. You will say just the right thing, not too much and not too little. Your downline will marvel at your ability to personally connect with their prospects.

However, as we explained in the previous chapter, we need to be careful about being *too* good. When we put the emphasis on being a great presenter or a great trainer, it makes the business all about how good *one person* can be. The key to this business is not you looking like an expert; the key is keeping things simple and duplicatable. When you show people the opportunity, they should think to themselves, *I think I can do that*. Remember that almost everyone who comes into this business has no sales experience and is not a public speaker. If you make the business look too hard, they will think *I could never do that in a million years!* Your business will suffer. Just ask Randy Gage:

I struggled in this business for five years. I bought tools. I bought products. I went to meetings. I invested, invested, and invested but I wasn't making money.

It started with not being able to get anyone to sign up. So, I said, "Okay, I need to learn how to sponsor people. That's the skill set I'm missing." I went out and learned how to do presentations. I started doing presentations literally five nights a week. I found a restaurant close to where I lived that had a banquet room in the back. So, five nights a week I was there with my *Miami Vice* suit, with my marker and my whiteboard drawing circles. And, I learned how to sponsor people.

I sponsored something like 30 people in a month. I thought, "Okay, they'll each get five people next month and that will be 150 and each of those 150 will get five and I'll have almost a thousand people after that second month. So, I'm ready to order the Lamborghini right away. Well, the next month rolls around and those 30 people, instead of turning into 150, turned into *three*; 27 of them dropped out. "No big deal," I said, "I'll just get 30 more."

And, that's what I did. I got out there with my *Miami Vice* suit, my marker and my whiteboard five nights a week. And, I sponsored another 30 or so. I did this for three or four months. The problem was I couldn't get people into the boat as quickly as they were jumping out of the boat.

The epiphany for me was realizing that I had created a process for bringing people into the business that no one could duplicate. To them, I was a star. I had to do all of the presentations. And, I did great presentations. That's how I became a professional speaker, by doing hundreds of network marketing meetings. I was saying, "Just bring your people to me. I'll sign them up for you." But, how do they duplicate that? They can't.

I realized that what I was doing was working—people *were* signing up—but it wasn't duplicating. I needed to bring people in in a way that allowed them to duplicate the process. That's when I started to use third-party tools, like videos, audios, flip charts, magazines, conference calls—anything that would take me out of the equation. So, now I'm simply pointing someone to a presentation; I'm *not* the presentation.

I still do public speaking. I think every leader in our profession does. But, when I have a new prospect, I'm never going to invite him to a presentation where I'm the speaker. Because, he's going to come up to me afterward and say, "You were great. You were really funny. I loved your stories. I know you'll be amazing at this. It's just not for me." That's because he can't see himself doing what I just did in front of hundreds of people; 9 out of 10 of us have a paralyzing fear of public speaking.

Instead, his first exposure might be me inviting him over to my house, where I put in a DVD and say, "Watch this and then let's talk about it." After that, he'll say, "Oh, so that's how you do the business? You invite people over to your house, play a DVD and answer questions? Well, I could do *that*."

And, when you do that some of them join and they invite people over to their house and they join and *bam!* you've really got something going. So, it's not about what works; it's about what duplicates.

Randy's experience makes it abundantly clear that we need to get out of the way and let The System do the work. Sometimes, a networker will intentionally seize the spotlight; other times she may not realize she is doing it at all. But, the signs that she is making it all about *her* are quite clear nonetheless:

1) She doesn't introduce her prospects to their future upline; she is the only one they ever talk to;
2) She feels the need to have the microphone in her hand at every public presentation;
3) She refers to her downline as "my distributors" instead of emphasizing that they are in business for themselves;
4) She takes credit for her downline's success, saying things like "I advanced them three levels in six months' time."

These are the kind of behaviors that kill duplication. The wise network marketer, however, knows how to step aside and use The System to duplicate herself. She knows that while not everyone can do a great presentation, everyone can find people, introduce them to the team and plug them in. To her, it doesn't matter who gets the credit as long as the teaching is being done.

Think of your job as being a connector: you connect your prospects to The System. That's what you do; *that's* pretty simple. Granted, there is a bit more to it than that, but we encourage you to always think of your business in its most simplistic form. You are a people connector. That's it.

It has been 20 years since Randy had his epiphany. Today, he earns a seven-figure annual income and resides in Miami Beach, Florida in an apartment overlooking Biscayne Bay and the Miami skyline. Randy has an organization of more than 200,000 people in some 60 countries around the world. You might say he has figured out this whole duplication thing.

You can do it, too. Keep it simple, connect people to The System and get out of the way.

Building Solid Residual Income

Let's say that as you are getting your business started, you establish a dozen or so customers who each place orders. Some of these customers continue to order month after month, long after you have stopped providing follow-up. This provides you some nice monthly income. You could even go so far as to call it "residual." In fact, we *did* refer to it as such earlier in this book. Technically, it is residual because it is income based on something you did in the past. (You developed a customer.)

But, true residual income—the kind that allows you to be financially free—won't come from your retail sales. Being financially free would require you to have thousands of customers, which in turn would require your sales efforts to be nothing short of herculean.

True residual income is the money you are paid when product is sold by your downline, not you. It's a royalty or override, and is a percentage of the total business volume of everyone in your organization.

That's why the goal in network marketing isn't to build a huge customer base, but to build a network. It is leveraging your time through not just your efforts, but the efforts of others.

Take a close look at your latest income statement from your company. How much of your check was true residual income and how much was from you selling products? If you have been in the business for a while and most of your check is still retail income, then you need to re-examine the way you do things. It would appear that you are looking for customers and not business leaders.

It all goes back to duplication: introducing people to the opportunity, casting a vision, helping them become leaders and teaching *them* to do the same. Put The System to work for you. Everything is in place; the table is set. You just need to bring people to the table.

Quick Review: Duplication Through The System

1) The System allows you to build your business while you are still learning the business.
2) The System is a power source. Plug people into it.
3) Instruct and model for your downline, but do not give them dictates. You will lose your best people.
4) Keep the business simple. When you complicate it, you make it hard for people to do.
5) Get out of the way. Keep the focus on the opportunity and The System and off of you.
6) To build residual income, you must build an organization of leaders. Selling product won't do it.

Exercise

1) Think about your business habits. What are you doing to plug into The System and promote healthy duplication? In contrast, do you have any habits that promote unhealthy duplication? If so, what can you do to change that?

My Healthy Habits –

My Unhealthy Habits –

2) Take a moment to reflect on your business. Are you business-focused or are you product-focused? Are you looking for customers or business leaders? Write down your three (3) favorite prospecting lines or "ice-breakers." What do these tell you about your business?

TEN

Marketing Your Business

In building your business, you have many marketing avenues available to you. Some are essential, while others are optional. They range from free to nominal in cost to very expensive. Elsewhere in this book we discussed basic marketing tools such as individual appointments, open meetings and in-home presentations. We won't rehash them here.

As we proceed, we remind you that if our discussion of marketing tools and methods differs from what you have been taught, we urge you to have a conversation with your upline. We do not want this book to be a source of confusion or discord in any way.

Telephone Service

If there is one indispensible tool in your networking toolbox, it is your telephone. You pretty much have to have one in this business. Remember that basically you are a people connector, and most of the time you will connect people by phone. You will need to introduce your prospects to your upline, who may live in another part of the country or elsewhere around the world.

Look for a calling plan that gives you unlimited long distance. You will be making countless long-distance calls and quite often these will be lengthy calls. Three-way calling is a must and call forwarding is very helpful while you are traveling. You might consider a voice over Internet protocol (VOIP) service. Many VOIP plans allow you to call foreign countries at no charge while offering the same sound quality and reliability as traditional phone services.

Your answering machine or voice mail greeting should be short and professional. Don't use your kids for this. Although it is very cute for Grandma to hear, it isn't appropriate for your business.

Three-Way Calls

One of the basic skills you need to master is how to do a three-way call. The three-way call is a powerful way to paint a bigger picture for your prospect and will prove indispensible to your business. Many networkers would argue—and we would agree with them—that the size of your business is proportional to the number of three-way calls you make. The more of them you do, the larger your business.

The participants on the call are you, your prospect (or new downline) and your upline. To make a three-way call your telephone must have three-way calling capability. Also, your phone service must have three-way calling as an available feature. Most phone companies now offer it with their standard calling plans, but you may need to pay a little extra for this service.

Here are some tips for doing an effective three-way call:

Pre-Arrange The Call

Don't try to catch your prospect on the fly. You should always try to schedule your next contact with a prospect before the current contact ends. You also need to give your upline plenty of notice. Don't expect that they will be available at your beck and call. They have their own business to run and they have a life outside that business.

The Order Matters

You initiate the call by getting one of the other participants on the line with you. We suggest that you call your prospect or downline first and then connect your upline. There are several reasons to do it this way. First, it builds anticipation for the prospect. Let's say that you are about to connect Christy, your prospect, to Beve, your upline. You should have already been promoting Beve by telling Christy something like, "You are going to *love* meeting Beve; she is so helpful and she has an incredible story!" Now, you let Christy's anticipation build just a bit more by getting her on the phone first.

Another reason you want to connect Beve second is that it sets her up properly as an expert who is willing to take time from her day to share some of her wisdom. This may sound like a minor detail, but it isn't. Let's suppose that you reverse the order, that you have Beve on the phone when you call your prospect, Christy. Now, the whole dynamic changes. Instead of setting up Beve as the expert, you and Beve are calling the prospect, almost like a solicitation. Christy's subconscious may tell her, "Wow, this person really wants me badly. She's calling me with her help already on the phone."

Do you see the difference? On the surface, the order in which you connect people may not seem like a big deal. But, it is. It sets the tone for the entire call.

Also, you will find that on many occasions your prospect will not be there to take your call at the appointed time. They get busy and forget, have an emergency or simply ignore your call. By calling the prospect first, your upline doesn't have to be on the phone while it rings and rings and rings without anyone ever picking up. Remember, your upline is busy, too. Be respectful of her time at all times.

SET THEM UP TO WIN

When you get your prospect and upline on the phone, you need to pave the way for your upline to do her job; you need to "set her up to win." You do this by reinforcing your upline's position as someone who is being generous and helpful. This is not to say you should put your upline on a pedestal. If you oversell her knowledge and success, your prospect won't be able to relate to her. The idea is that you want the prospect to understand why they are on the phone, which is to learn and be inspired.

So, you might say something like this: "Christy, I am so glad that we were able to connect with Beve, because you will really appreciate what she has to say. She has been a great mentor and friend to me and now that you're getting a chance to talk with her, I think you'll see why I feel that way." Do you see how that sets Beve up to win? She can now connect with Christy from a position of strength.

What if, on the other hand, you tell Beve what a great person Christy is? For instance, "Beve, this is my friend Christy. She and I go way back, all the way to high school. Christy was always so popular and all the guys thought she was so pretty. She works at a floral shop and you know, I've always thought that would be so cool to make arrangements and do all the creative stuff that florists get to do. Anyway, Beve I'd like you to meet Christy."

Now, look what you've done. You've just told Beve (and Christy) how great Christy is and how exciting and fun her job is. And, if Christy's current situation is so great, why on earth would she want to look at your business? Anything Beve says from this point will have all the impact of a wet firecracker.

Similarly, don't say to your prospect, "This is Beve. She'd like to tell you more about the business and what it's done for her." Well, who cares what Beve *would like?* Did you really call Christy just so Beve could tell her how great her life is? You have essentially told the prospect that she is doing you (and Beve) a favor by listening.

And, while it may be true that Beve wants to share her story with your prospect—she is helping you build your business, after all—that is not the point of the call. The point is not what Beve gets to tell; rather, it is what Christy gets to hear. This is an opportunity for Christy to gather information that will advance her toward making a decision about the business.

BE QUIET

Once you introduce Christy and Beve, you need to get out of the way. Be quiet and let them connect. For new distributors, this can be a challenge. They get nervous or think they need to manage the conversation. Sooner or later they start talking. You must resist the urge to interject. Mentally, you need to take a seat at another table; watch but don't participate. This is your upline's time to connect with your prospect, to begin to establish a relationship. Let that relationship happen.

Another benefit of taking yourself out of the conversation is that you can let your upline ask the questions that you are hesitant to ask. Perhaps you are afraid to ask the prospect for a decision: *Do they see themselves doing this business?* While Beve is getting to know Christy, she can ask that question for you.

But, for this to work effectively, you need to stay out of the way. Let your upline connect with the prospect and don't break the connection by adding your two cents to the conversation.

Ending The Call

At the end of the call, do NOT thank Christy. Remember what we said earlier about thanking the prospect. You are doing her a favor, not the other way around. You *should*, however, thank Beve. Reinforce to your prospect that it was a privilege to have your upline take time from her day to talk with the two of you.

Before you hang up, you will want to set your next contact with the prospect. You may also have some other things to discuss with her, particularly if she is a good friend. But, before you do any of this, excuse your upline from the call. Don't take up more of her time while you set another appointment or chit-chat.

Get Feedback

Once your upline is off the phone, take a moment to validate her again. Say something like, "Isn't Beve great? She has a great story, doesn't she?" This helps cement the relationship Beve is building with your prospect.

You should also ask Christy what she thought about the call. Hopefully, she gave plenty of feedback during her conversation with Beve, but this gives her the opportunity to say more. There may be things that she was not comfortable sharing with Beve but will tell you. Perhaps Beve inadvertently said something that Christy didn't like. Christy may share that with you privately, and in turn you can pass it along to Beve who should talk to Christy again to clear up any misunderstanding.

Conference Calls

When you need to speak to several people at once and you can't all be in one place, conference calls are the next best thing to being there. A conference call consists of a "host" who leads the call, and participants—

there might be 5 or 500—who listen. Some of them may also speak at appointed times.

Conference calls are a convenient way to introduce people to your upline when you have several new downline in your organization all joining at the same time. You should also include prospects. Conference calls can create quite a buzz, much like an open meeting.

Be sure to have people introduce themselves and where they are from as they join the conference line. Having your prospect hear people calling in from all over the country adds a powerful dynamic to the experience. Once you have introduced yourself, observe proper etiquette by muting your line. Nothing is more distracting to other listeners than hearing you yell instructions to the kids or your television or blender blaring in the background.

Most conference services have a feature that allows you to record and archive your calls so people can dial in and listen at a later time. Many services even offer an audio file that can be downloaded and played on a computer, transferred to an mp3 player or burned to a CD.

The best part about conference call services is that many of them are free—no catches or conditions; they are 100 percent free of charge. Companies give these services away in hope that you will purchase other products they offer. If you do an Internet search for "free conference call" you will find several. Do a little research on each company and read some consumer reviews before selecting one.

Brochures

Printed materials can be helpful, but also pricey. Exercise caution when using brochures, flyers and other similar marketing pieces. In most cases, they are beautifully and professionally done, but having a nice looking brochure is only effective if the prospect reads it.

And, in most cases they won't, particularly if you are giving them out like dinner mints. Remember, only a small percentage of your prospects will buy your product or join your business. So, if you give a brochure to every prospect, where do most of these materials go? They get tossed into the trash without the prospect ever reading them.

Some people will argue that this is just part of the cost of doing business. To an extent, that is true; however, no one says you have to waste money. Assume that you are talking to a prospect who lives 500 miles away and he says, "Send me some information and I'll get back to you." Is it worth the money you are going to spend on the brochure, plus the packaging, the postage and the gasoline to drive to the post office? Is the prospect serious, or is he just asking for more information as a polite way of ending the call? Most of the time, it is the latter.

A few chapters back we discussed why (and how) you should qualify your prospects. And now, we've just given you another good reason why you should do it. Before you hand out that brochure, qualify your prospect. Don't waste your time and money. We are not saying you should never use printed materials; however, we *are* advising that you use discretion.

Incentives

A popular sales technique in the corporate world is to offer the prospect a free meal, a round of golf, a gift basket or some other incentive to make a purchase or attend a presentation. And, while this is widely accepted in the traditional marketplace, we highly recommend that you not do these things.

Incentives might be appropriate if you are selling cars, insurance policies or satellite television service. But, do you really need to entice your prospect into buying your product or joining your business? We think not. You are selling them an opportunity to change their future, not a premium movie channel. Your goal is a relationship, not a sale.

If you have a booth at a fair or trade show and you do a drawing for a free gas card as a means of collecting contact information, then okay. That's much different than paying someone to look at your opportunity.

If you go to lunch with your prospect, pay your own meal and expect that he will, too. The same goes for a round of golf or a concert.

Remember that the opportunity you are offering is a gift; it is its own prize. Don't cheapen it by offering incentives.

The Cold Market

At some point in your business, you may consider working the cold market and when you do, you will have many options. There is advertising (radio, television, billboards, newspapers, magazines and other periodicals), websites, banner ads and capture pages on the Internet, purchased leads, yard signs, magnetic signs for your car and other avenues too numerous to mention.

Some groups frown on advertising and instead teach their downline to build their business exclusively through their hot and warm markets and opportune moments, such as meeting people at a coffee shop or in line at the grocery store. Their reasoning is:

1) you will have a higher level of comfort and therefore a higher rate of success with people you already know;

2) your credibility with someone you know is much higher than with a stranger;

3) advertising subjects you to an extremely high rate of "No's," which can be very discouraging to the unseasoned networker;

4) advertising can be very expensive and eat up all of your business profit (or worse, cause you to run up high amounts of debt); and

5) the cost coupled with the high rate of "rejection" may cause you to quit.

Other groups embrace the cold market, citing the following:

1) advertising is an accepted and well-established business practice;

2) you have to spend money to make money; and

3) advertising allows you to cast a wider net and reach more people compared to your hot and warm markets.

We are not going to tell you that you should work the cold market, nor are we going to tell you that you shouldn't. We recommend that you discuss the issue with your upline and get their input and advice before making a decision. They have the experience and knowledge to advise you on doing it properly, and probably know what works and what doesn't.

ARE YOU PREPARED FOR THIS?

Before you venture into the cold market, we strongly urge you to consider the cost. Set a budget and commit to not exceeding it. Most of us are deeply invested emotionally in our network marketing businesses. In our zeal to find our next leader we can spend our way into a huge mess if we aren't careful.

We also recommend you "shadow" someone who is already doing it. Ask if you can listen in. How are they engaging their prospects? How do they qualify them? How do they take the prospect through the Invitation, Presentation and Follow-Up steps? These are all things that you should work out in advance, and if possible observe first-hand.

Also, consider your motive for advertising. Is it fear? Let's be frank: many people prefer advertising over working their hot market because they fear alienating their friends and family or being ridiculed. *Lookout, here comes Pyramid Pete! Everybody run!*

Fear of rejection is a very powerful thing. Many of us will spend hundreds of dollars on advertising if we believe it will make people *come to us* instead of having to pick up the phone. So, before you spend any money on advertising, give some honest thought to why you are doing it.

Why? Because if you have fear about talking to people you already know, you probably aren't as prepared as you think to talk to people you *don't* know. Remember, this is the cold market. We have already explained that it's called "cold" for a reason. When you advertise, a majority of your prospects who respond via email will disappear after that first contact. You will never hear from them again, despite your repeated attempts to reach them.

Many of the people who respond via telephone will be highly skeptical but also curious (or desperate) enough to call anyway. They will think that because they don't know you, they can say or do anything. They will be impatient, rude, guarded and largely uncooperative. Some will hang up on you.

That's the cold market, folks. It's like opening your front door and getting a blast of frigid winter air smack in the face. And, once you've had your fill of no-shows, hang-ups, jerks and people who are genuinely shocked to learn they might actually have to do some work—*You mean I can't just watch TV all day in my underwear and make money?*—the thought of calling your best friend may not be so scary after all.

Newspaper & Magazine Advertising

With the advent of the Internet, the printed versions of newspapers and magazines are not as relevant as they used to be. In fact, some daily newspapers are printing only on Sundays and others have gone completely online.

But, whereas printed publications are not the advertising heavyweight they used to be, people do still read them. Here are some things to consider when placing ads in newspapers and magazines:

PUBLICATION CYCLE

Most large newspapers are published daily, whereas smaller ones might be weekly. Most magazines are monthly. Keep in mind that with daily publications, people have one chance to see your ad: the day it is published. It is "here today, gone tomorrow."

Weekly and monthly publications, however, have a longer "shelf life," meaning people tend to hold onto them longer (in some cases until the next edition is published). This increases the chance that your ad will be seen more than once, on more than one day by more than one person. This is especially true when the publication is in the lobby of an office building where there is high traffic. The drawback is that weekly and monthly publications typically do not have as large a circulation as those printed daily.

CIRCULATION

As a rule of thumb, the larger a publication's circulation the higher the cost to advertise. For instance, an ad in the *New York Times* will cost you a lot more than a weekly paper in rural Iowa. However, be advised that just because a publication is distributed (or "circulated") doesn't mean it is actually read.

Unlike most large newspapers (which charge for a subscription and deliver right to your door), many small newspapers are free. They are distributed through racks at grocery stores, banks, coffee shops, restaurants and so on. The fact that the publication is distributed widely (say, 50,000 copies per week) does not mean that it is widely read. Before you place an ad in any publication—daily or monthly, paid or free—

ask if the publisher has audited the readership. In other words, can they tell you who is reading their publication and how often?

In most cases, small publications do not audit their readership; it's expenseive and they simply cannot afford to do it. You should always consider readership (as opposed to circulation); however, don't dismiss a publication just because they cannot tell you what their readership is. At a minimum, by asking the question you demonstrate to the salesperson that you are more educated than the average media buyer.

RESTRICTIONS

Many newspapers require that your ad clearly state that you are offering a business opportunity, not a job. Even if they don't require this, you should not lead people to believe they are responding to a job opening. You should never mislead people. For this reason, many newspapers will not allow you to post your ad in the Help Wanted section. Some publications will not accept business opportunity ads at all.

ONLINE EDITIONS

Most newspapers and magazines now have online editions to complement their printed publication. They will likely offer you incentives to advertise in both printed and online versions. Study your options carefully; consider if it makes sense to advertise in one or the other, or both. Again, ask if the online edition of the newspaper has been audited for readership. In the next chapter, we will discuss banner advertising. All of the points we make there apply here as well.

Radio Advertising

As with printed editions of newspapers and magazines, the relevance of broadcast radio has diminished somewhat. More and more people are using mp3 players to listen to music and downloading their news and information via podcasts from the Internet. However, radio remains a viable advertising force and is typically a great value.

SCHEDULE

When your radio advertisement airs is critical. The peak of radio listenership is morning and afternoon "drive time," when people are in their cars commuting to and from work. Naturally, these are the most expensive time slots you can buy. If you are targeting professionals who might see your opportunity as a way to escape from the corporate "rat race," then you definitely want to place your ads (also called "spots") during drive time.

If you are targeting a different demographic, such as stay-at-home moms, drive time is not as important. Moms may be listening at home or even more likely to hear your ad in their car as they run errands throughout the day.

Understand the term "ROS" and how it affects your advertising. "ROS" stands for *Run Of Schedule* and means that your spot is not designated for any particular time slot. Instead, it will air at various times throughout the station's broadcast schedule, wherever there is an open slot remaining. It is done at the convenience of the radio station. ROS spots are typically sold in blocks at a discounted rate because your spot can be bumped out of a prime time slot by another advertiser who is paying to be there.

REACH & FREQUENCY

Radio listenership is measured by *frequency* and *reach*. Reach is the number (or percentage) of people in the broadcast area who listen to that radio station. Frequency is the number of times those people will hear your spot during your advertising campaign.

A long-standing rule of thumb in the industry is that listeners need to hear your spot multiple times before they take action. That could be two times or it could be two *hundred* times; it all depends on the listener. Marketing strategists will also say that frequency is more important than reach. It's not how many people hear your spot, but how many *times* they hear it. In other words, it's better to cast a smaller net several times than cast a big net once.

DEMOGRAPHIC TARGETING

Radio is very effective at targeting demographics and is probably surpassed only by the Internet in terms of reaching selected population groups.

Why is this helpful? Well, say for instance that the typical person who joins your business is a female age 35-55, who has children at home and has a professional vocation. To reach that demographic, you will want to advertise on the station that has the highest concentration of that population in its listenership. Find out which stations—more specifically, which *programs* on those stations—your target audience is listening to, and place your advertising there. The sales staff at the radio station will gladly provide you with a breakdown of which demographics are listening and when.

CATCHING SALES

Do some research and find out when your local radio station typically has sales or other promotions. For instance, the first quarter of the year (January through March) is traditionally slow for radio stations. Retailers have just spent heavily on advertising during the Christmas season and have scaled back their advertising for the next several months. As a result, advertising is usually cheaper during the first quarter because the demand is low.

It just so happens that this is a good time for you to advertise. People aren't thinking about the holidays or summer vacations, but they *are* thinking about New Year's resolutions and your opportunity might just be their answer.

Television

We're not going to say much about television advertising. It is generally very expensive and beyond the economic reach of most network marketers. Moreover, while television is a very effective medium for selling a product, it is not as effective as a recruitment tool. The bottom line is that other media are a much better value than television when it comes to advertising your opportunity. If you are considering television advertising, check your distributor agreement first. Some companies strictly forbid this form of advertising.

Toll-Free Number & Voicemail

When you run an advertisement that features a phone number, it is best to have that call go to a live person instead of a voicemail. (Don't you find automated answering systems a bit annoying?) If you are available to take your prospect's call, the chance of advancing him is much greater than if he gets a recording.

If you are hesitant to publish your phone number, you can purchase a toll-free number and have it privately forward to your cell phone or business line. Do an online search for toll-free number services and you will find many from which to choose. Most charge a base rate plus a charge for each incoming call. The more calls you receive, the larger your bill. Although most people today have unlimited long-distance calling on their cell phones and land lines, some of your prospects may not. It is considerate of you to offer them a toll-free number.

For those times when you are not available to take the calls, you may want to consider a stand-alone voicemail. This is a voicemail service that is independent from your cell phone, home phone or business line. Like the toll-free number, you will find many companies online that offer voicemail services. Many will combine a toll-free number and voicemail in one package. Most charge a basic rate plus additional charges for each minute of voicemail received.

Some features you may want to look for:

- *Caller ID* – This is handy for following up with callers who don't leave a message.
- *Audio files* – You receive an email with the prospect's message attached as an audio file. This is particularly helpful if you have several distributors sharing leads from one advertising campaign. You simply forward the email to the appropriate distributor and in addition to a name and telephone number, they can actually hear the caller's message.

Purchased Leads

Purchased leads are names and contact information of people who have indicated that they may be interested in what you are selling. Purchased leads are used in many industries. For example, insurance and financial services agents buy leads as a means for finding clients. Doctors and dentists use them to find patients, and general contractors buy leads to find people who are considering a kitchen or bathroom remodel. Network marketers buy leads, too.

Leads are collected and sold by lead-generating companies that put ads on the Internet. In the network marketing arena, these ads will typically say "work from home" or something similar. The ads feature a contact form. When someone fills out and submits the form, their information is sold to a network marketer.

Purchased leads have a strong allure for many reasons:

1) *It saves time.* Who isn't busy today? For people who have money to spend but precious little time, buying leads might make sense.

2) *We don't know how to prospect.* Most of us who join network marketing don't have sales and marketing experience and we don't have a clue when it comes to prospecting. Quite simply, we don't know how to talk to people. Striking up conversations at coffee shops, the grocery store or post office doesn't come naturally. Paying someone to bring people to us is a lot easier.

3) *We've exhausted our hot market*; or so we think. When we've talked to everyone on our list (or at least everyone we're not too chicken to call), paying for leads is a natural next step.

4) *We fear rejection.* This is the biggie. A lot of us buy leads because the thought of someone we know and respect telling us "No" is more than we can bear. So, we buy leads with the assumption that because the prospect filled out a contact form somewhere on the Internet, he is at least *somewhat* interested. And, that's good enough. If they say "No," well at least they came to us and we didn't have to pester them. Besides, we don't even know them so who cares if they don't like us?

If you have purchased leads before, what we are going to tell you next will be no surprise. However, if you have never purchased leads this may come as a shock: a vast majority of the leads—in some cases nearly 100 percent—will not join your business.

That's right. Almost all of the leads you buy will be a dead end. You will get people who are:

1) *Not available* – You will never be able to reach them; they won't answer your calls or respond to your email.

2) *Not serious* – They filled out the contact form at 2:00 a.m. when they couldn't sleep or they were mad at their boss but now they're over it.

3) *Not qualified* – They lack the money or the skills to do your business, or both.

Understand, too, that you may not be the only person buying that particular lead. Many leads are sold multiple times (although you can buy "exclusive" leads). So, don't be surprised if your prospect says, "You're the tenth person who's called me. I'm tired of this!"

Still, you will have the occasional person join your team and for that reason, many network marketers are willing to spend a lot of money and go through hundreds or thousands of dead leads to find one leader.

Here are some questions to ask before purchasing leads:

1) *How are the leads captured?* Ask to see a capture page. This is the website where the prospect fills out the contact form.

2) *Are the leads exclusive or are they sold numerous times?* If they are sold more than once, how often?

3) *How soon after it is "captured" is the lead distributed?* You wouldn't buy old produce and you shouldn't buy old leads. The person may no longer be interested, or may have already joined another company.

4) *Are the leads pre-screened?* This is an added feature where the lead-generating company contacts the prospect to verify that they are indeed interested *and* qualified. These leads cost a lot more.

It All Comes Back To Relationships

We have given you many insights on the various advertising tools available to you. Hopefully, you are now armed with information that will help you make wise choices in your advertising efforts.

We want to leave you with one more point, and it's an important one: advertising alone will not build your business. It is a way to prospect, a way to introduce yourself to people. It is a tool; nothing more, nothing less.

You still have to go through the Invitation, Presentation and Follow-Up steps we outlined for you earlier. You have to do the work. It's a misguided notion to think that that running a newspaper ad or throwing a website up on the Internet is going to build your business. It won't.

People don't follow products, advertisements cr websites. People follow people. Marketing tools may get someone's attention, but they don't make the sale. That's your job. It all comes back to you developing relationships and molding leaders.

Quick Review: Marketing Your Business

1) On three-way calls, set your helper up to win. Edify them, not the prospect. Be quiet and let your helper build rapport.
2) Incentives cheapen your opportunity. Don't use them.
3) Conference calls can be a powerful tool for showing your prospect a bigger picture of your opportunity.
4) Monitor your use of printed materials. Are they effective or just a waste of money?
5) Working the cold market is very difficult. It is also expensive. Don't jump into advertising until you know what you are doing, and maybe not even then.
6) Marketing tools are just tools; they won't build your business for you. You still have to make the sale.

Exercise

1) Role play a three-way call with your upline or another networker. First, do everything the wrong way, the exact opposite of what we have taught you. Then, do the call the proper way, setting your upline up to win. How were the dynamics different between the two approaches? In what ways was the set-up for the second call more effective?

ELEVEN

Harnessing The Internet

The World Wide Web has changed us in ways too numerous to list. One could argue that there is not one facet of life that has not been impacted in some way by the Internet. Certainly, its influence on business has been dramatic.

Today, more than 2 billion people—roughly 1 in 3 on the planet—use the Internet.[1] At the end of 2011, there were some 555 million websites worldwide, *more than double the amount that existed the year before.* The world is becoming smaller day by day, the distance between us shrinking rapidly. We can communicate with more people more immediately than ever before.

The Internet is great for your business because people can get information quickly and easily. The Internet is *bad* for your business because people can get information quickly and easily. The Internet is great because it validates your opportunity, is convenient and immediate. But, it is also unregulated and prone to misinformation and deceptive practice.

It Validates Your Opportunity

The Internet has become our *de facto* source for information; it's where we go first when we need to know just about anything. So, when you are talking to a prospect their first question is usually "What's your website?" (not, "Do you have one?"). People expect to find you on the web and when they arrive at your professional looking website it validates you and your opportunity. *OK, this must be for real. Here's their website.* If, however, you don't have a website (or you have one that is poorly done) it will be hard for you to be taken seriously. Right or wrong, not having a presence on the web makes you look second-rate and outdated.

It Is Convenient & Immediate

The Internet is also helpful because of its convenience. You don't have to fight traffic and drive across town to meet with a prospect (although we encourage you to meet with prospects in person when possible). A well-designed website featuring information crafted just for your prospect can greatly enhance your recruitment of them.

The Internet is immediate and makes doing business outside your geographical area much easier. Your prospects can instantly learn about your opportunity—again, by going to your website. They don't have to wait for the post office to deliver a brochure or magazine that you mailed them. You can use the website to do the appointment while the two of you talk on the phone.

The Internet has also made ordering product much easier. Gone are the days when your customers had to call you (or the company) to place their order. Now, most companies feature online ordering that customers can do on their own at their convenience.

It Is Unregulated

The impact of the Internet on the network marketing industry is not all good. Your prospects can easily find half-truths and distortions about network marketing *and your company* posted all over the Internet.

Unfortunately, the Internet has become the world's new bathroom wall: anybody can write anything. The result is that you will lose some prospects because of this. In some cases, you can educate your prospect and alleviate their fears. But, if you can't, don't fret about it. A lot of prospects are just looking for a reason to say "No" and the negative stuff they read on the web gives them what they want: an excuse to stay where they are in life.

You must also understand that with information now available at the click of a mouse, it is much harder to keep control of the prospecting process. It is quite likely that while you are talking to a prospect on the phone for the first time, they will be "Googling" your company for information and only partially listening to what you are saying.

Such is the reality of the Internet: it validates, it is convenient and it is immediate, but also cluttered with material better suited for a public restroom. In the balance of this chapter, we will help you make sense of it all and give you tips on how you can harness the power of the World Wide Web.

Your Website

When it comes to the Internet, the thought process of the typical network marketer is something like: "I'll get a website, be on the front page of Google and people will find me and sign up." Wouldn't that be great? Oh, if it was just that easy!

The reality is that being on the front page of Google can be very expensive and therefore beyond the reach of most network marketers. A high search engine position is a result of many factors, and is a complicated and highly competitive process. Today, you can find literally hundreds of companies that offer search engine optimization (SEO).

"Search engine optimization is not magic," says SEO expert Michael Lee Joshua. "It is tedious, detailed work that must be diligently performed if you want to attract new visitors and build a solid customer base."[2]

Paying for a Top 10 results position on Google will likely cost you well into four figures (or substantially more) for a very competitive keyword or keyphrase. It is a big, big business. Nevertheless, it might be helpful for you to have a basic understanding of how SEO works. The search engines—Google, Yahoo! and Bing are the major ones—rank websites on a variety of factors. We are going to give you a few of them, but understand that this is a simple list and by no means an exhaustive analysis of the process:

- *Inbound links* – This is the number of other websites that link to yours. The more inbound links to your site, the higher your ranking. The quality and relevance of the websites that link to your site are also a factor.

- *Time* – Newer websites don't rank as high as those that have been around a while.
- *Updates* – Websites that are static and rarely (if ever) updated don't rank as high as those that have frequently updated content.
- *Content* – The more thorough and valuable your content is to the public, the more visitors you will attract. Having more visitors leads to your pages being rewarded with higher results positions.
- *Keywords/Keyphrases* – Keywords and keyphrases are common terms used by people when they do searches (for instance, "work from home"). When you use keywords and keyphrases on your website that match what people are searching for (and if these accurately reflect your content), you will be rewarded by a better search engine results position. If you use keywords and keyphrases that don't reflect your content but are just a lure to attract visitors, the search engines will not only ignore your site, but will probably penalize your site by devaluing it.
- *Popularity* – A page on a website that is visited frequently will have a higher search position than a similar page on a competing website that has not been viewed as often. In other words, the more popular your page is the higher it will be ranked.

What Search Engines Think Of Your Website

Now that you understand a little about how search engines work, let's consider how they rank the typical network marketer's website. And, the answer is: not very high. By and large, network marketer's personal websites do not rank well on search engine queries.

For starters, if you have a website supplied by your company it is most likely a replicated template. In other words, it has the same look and same content as the hundreds of other websites your company has provided for its distributors. Only your name and contact information (and perhaps your photo and bio) differentiate your website from the next person's. When search engines see the same content on multiple websites, they may downgrade the rank of every one of those sites.

Second, the content tends to be static and is updated infrequently. Third, your website is probably not optimized in the placement and frequency of keywords. And last, there is a good bet that few websites (if any) elsewhere on the Internet are linking to yours.

So, if you have the average network marketing website, don't expect to be on the front page of Google when someone searches for "work from home." In fact, unless you are willing and able to invest a lot of money and time, don't expect to be anywhere in the first *100* pages.

Even if someone specifically searches on your company's name, your chances are not much better. You are competing with your parent company's website and that of every other fellow distributor. Plus, *all* of you are competing against people who invest a lot of time and money in optimizing their search engine rank. For instance, do a search of your company's name. In the top 10 results, you will likely find websites warning people about "scams" and "complaints" associated with your company. These websites often tout a competing product or some type of training or marketing system. Some of them just want you to visit because it increases their advertising revenue. They have nothing whatsoever to do with your company. The people who own these websites know that your prospects will be searching your company name and this is their attempt to distract or influence them.

Perhaps you find all of this quite discouraging, especially if you have let yourself believe that "all I have to do is put up a website and people will find me." Sorry to burst your bubble; it just doesn't work that way. We want you to be informed and we want you to have realistic expectations. But, we also don't want you to be discouraged.

The Real Value Of Your Website

Though your website may not harvest lots of prospects, it can still be a fantastic asset. We suggest you focus on using it as a validation tool for people you have already engaged. In other words, don't think of your website as a prospecting tool, but rather a *presentation* tool. That's probably how it's designed, anyway.

If your website is typical of most in the industry, it has sections that talk about your products, your company, your business opportunity and yourself. You will have a contact page as well.

Think about this: aren't those also the basic parts of your company's brochure, presentation booklet or the slide show used at an open meeting? Don't these also contain a section on the products, the company and the business opportunity? The only real difference is that your website also has a little information about you.

So, your website is really just a presentation tool, like your brochure or slide show. It just happens to be on the Internet. And, just like you have to talk to your prospects prior to them coming to the appointment or open meeting, you will have to talk to people to get them to your website. You may get a few prospects by simply having a presence online, but by and large the benefit of your website will come *after* you have engaged the prospect.

Internet Ads

On the Internet, you have many choices when it comes to advertising. There are banner ads, text ads, rich media ads (those that have sound and animation) and pop-up ads, to name a few. The number of options and the differences between them can be confusing to even the most knowledgeable of Internet users and downright overwhelming for those who aren't web savvy. Here are a few pointers on understanding Internet advertising:

IMPRESSIONS VERSUS CLICK-THROUGHS

Most Internet advertising is sold as either "impressions" or "click-throughs." A click-through means that someone clicked on your ad and was connected to your website. An impression, on the other hand, occurs each time your ad appears on a webpage that is being viewed by someone. Whether or not that person clicks on your ad—much less, whether or not they even *notice* it—is irrelevant. The fact that the ad is there while the page is being viewed, counts as an impression.

Since impressions cannot guarantee that anyone will connect to your website, they are much cheaper than click-throughs. Retailers and other companies that are looking to build brand recognition may prefer impressions, because they can get their name in front of a lot of people for less money. However, your goal is different: you want to engage people, one-on-one. For this reason, you will probably want to purchase click-throughs.

In most cases, you pay in advance for your ads regardless of which type they are. That gives you a "bank account," so to speak. Each time your ad is displayed or clicked on, money is taken out of your account. When your account is empty, your ad is taken down from the website.

Some contracts, however, are open-ended. In other words, they keep your ad active and charge your credit card for it until you tell them to stop. As a result, you could quickly find yourself having spent much more than you anticipated. Before you purchase Internet advertising, do your homework. Be sure that you understand the terms of the contract.

PLACEMENT

You should also pay attention to where your ad is displayed on the website. How many other ads are on the same page with yours? Is the page so jammed with ads that yours gets lost in the mix? Also, ask if your ad will appear "above the fold." This is an old newspaper term referring to whether the ad is placed above or below where the newspaper is folded. Ads above the fold are typically viewed more and therefore more desirable. On the Internet, the "fold" is the bottom of the screen. Your ad may not appear on the screen immediately, but instead require that the website visitor scroll down in order to see it. The fact that the visitor accessed the page counts as an impression, regardless of whether or not he scrolled to the bottom.

The number of ads on the page and the placement of your ad on the page are of particular importance if you are buying impressions as opposed to click-throughs.

FLAT-RATE ADS

If you are purchasing an ad for a flat rate—in other words, you are paying a certain amount per month, without respect to impressions or click-throughs—there are some additional things to consider.

For starters, how much traffic does the website get? Moreover, how much traffic goes to the *page* that your ad is on? The website owner may be promoting the fact that his website gets 100,000 hits a month, but that doesn't do you any good if the page your ad is on gets only 50 views per month.

You should also pay attention to how much editorial content is on the page where your ad is displayed. Editorial content is everything that is not advertising, such as feature articles, opinion pieces and news. Since people go to the Internet looking for information, you generally want your ad to be on a page that contains editorial content. Your goal is for people to notice your ad while they are there searching for something else. Some web pages are 100 percent advertising; a "business partner directory" is one example. If only business partners are listed on this page, it is highly likely that your exposure will be limited to only those people who are interested in seeing who the business partners are.

If you are purchasing impressions or click-throughs, these concerns are not as great. Remember, you are only charged when your ad is clicked-on or when it appears on a viewed page.

Search Advertising

The last time you did a search on the Internet using any of the common search engines, no doubt you noticed the text ads that appeared to the right of the search results. You also saw within your search results a few of them at the very top of the page, probably with a slightly different color background. The text ads to the right and the ones at the top of your search results are called "search advertising." In other words, the ads that appear are based on the keywords you used in your search query. Say, for instance, that you do a search for "how to select the right computer." When your search results are returned, you will see numerous text ads beckoning you to visit websites where you can buy computers.

Search advertising accounts for nearly half of all Internet advertising.[3] In addition to appearing on search engines, search advertising can be found on most websites and blogs that feature ads. Google's AdWords are the most popular,[4] with Yahoo! Search Marketing, Microsoft adCenter, AOL and Facebook also serving as major players in the online ad arena.

Search advertising is alluring because it enables you to target people who might be looking for answers to a particular problem that your product or business opportunity can address. But, it is also pricey. The fact that Google routinely gives away $100 in AdWord advertising as an incentive to would-be customers should give you an indication of how expensive these ads can be.

Webinars

"Webinar" is a combination of the terms "web-based" and "seminar." Webinars are seminars that are done online. Imagine taking an open meeting to the Internet. Instead of coming to a hotel or someone's house, people log onto a website where they see the same presentation.

Most webinar services come with a fee, but a few are free. The free services are generally ad-supported, meaning you will see advertisements on the side of your screen when you attend the webinar. The revenue generated by the advertising allows the webinar company to offer the service for free. Many of the free services have limitations, such as the number of participants per webinar, but still have plenty of features that make them worth checking out.

When researching webinar service, here are some things to consider:

- *Number of attendees* – What is the maximum allowable?
- *Number of presenters* – Can there be more than one?
- *VOIP* – Can you broadcast your voice over the Internet instead of people having to call in on a conference line?
- *Media capability* – Can you use video? Is there a whiteboard function?
- *Chat feature* – Is there chat capability for asking questions?
- *Record enabled* – Can you record and archive the webinar?
- *Scheduling and sign-up* – Can the webinar be scheduled in advance?
- *Pause transmission* – Can you pause the webinar?
- *Real-time transmission* – Is there lag time or can the presentation be viewed in real time?
- *Platform compatibility* – Can it be viewed on both PC and Mac?

- *Free standing* – Do participants have to download any software or is the service free standing?
- *Branding* – Can you insert your company's logo?
- *Reports* – Will the service generate attendance and other reports?
- *Support* – Is technical support available should you have problems?

Attraction Marketing

Since the very beginning of network marketing, the formula for building the business has been pretty constant: make a list of people you know, contact them and show the opportunity to those who are interested. In the past several decades, not much has changed.

However, fueled by the popularity of the Internet, a new approach is gaining steam in the marketplace: attraction marketing. Attraction marketing is, essentially, getting people to come to *you* instead of you going to them.

It's somewhat like a manufacturer giving away coupons for a free sample of their product. Let's say the product is laundry detergent. The manufacturer hopes that you will use their free sample, like it, and because of your positive experience will be inclined to purchase their product in the future. The intent of the free sample is to impact your choice the next time you need laundry detergent, and ultimately to build brand loyalty.

With attraction marketing, the goal isn't to sell a product, but to build a relationship. You use an enticement to attract the prospect, but in this case it's not a free sample. Remember that most of us go to the Internet looking for information; we want answers to our questions. So, your enticement is free information; you give people the answers they are looking for.

Let's examine how this might work in a traditional business. Let's say you own an athletic apparel company. What if instead of placing ads that talk about how great your running shoes are (which is probably what your competitors are doing), you gave out free information on how to select a shoe that is best for your age and body type, the importance of warming up before exercise or the keys to an effective workout?

If you own a vehicle repair shop, in addition to running Internet ads about your oil change special why not give tips on getting better gas mileage or reducing wear on a car's brakes or tires?

Let's say you own an organic foods store. You could feature a recipe of the week. People who shop for organic foods are likely interested in conservation and recycling, as well. You might offer them tips on reducing the use of water in their home or creating less waste.

When you provide information that is both free and valuable, people are naturally attracted to you. If you provide a place for them to give you their contact information (email address or phone number, for instance), you have an opportunity to build a relationship with those who want even more information. Having a free newsletter, for example, delivered right to their email inbox, is a great way to do this. The more you cultivate the relationship, the greater the chance they will become your customer.

Essentially, you are telling the prospective customer, "I am providing useful information to you for free and I am willing to continue to do this without asking for anything in return, ever." This makes you extremely likeable—and different; while everyone else is trying to sell them something, you are helping them solve a problem by giving free help. That is savvy marketing.

Of course, you can also use attraction marketing in your networking business. And, for a majority of us in this industry, the most effective and most economical way to do this is through a blog.

Blogs

The term "blog" is short for "weblog," which draws its name from "World Wide Web" and "log," or written record. Blogs are a way for the writer to share his or her thoughts about a particular topic with the world. Blogs can be factual reports, opinion pieces or a combination of the two.

If you like to write, you might consider starting a blog for your business. Blogs lend themselves extremely well to attraction marketing, because they give you an opportunity to educate your prospects. David Meerman Scott, author and marketing expert, offers great advice on how to do this. "The first thing you need to do," he says, "is put away your company hat for a moment and think like one of your buyer(s)..."[5]

In other words, think about what they want to hear, not what you want to tell them. This is counterintuitive to what we've been taught, which is "just be excited and tell everybody" about our business and products. And, whereas that is still a good face-to-face strategy, in the online world it doesn't work. Remember that people are on the web looking for information, for answers to their problems. You need to talk about what's on *their* mind, not yours.

For instance, prospects for your business opportunity might be interested in such things as leadership, motivation or setting goals. You might also write about work-life balance, business trends, how people are turning to a part-time business to fund their retirement or how a business is insurance against job loss. You could even discuss how a home-based business offers tax advantages.

If you are a distributor for a nutritional company, you might blog about how major diseases are diet related, why our foods don't have the nutritional value they used to or how exercise can fit into even the busiest of schedules.

Suppose you are with a company that offers financial services. You might write about being prepared for retirement, the Top 10 mistakes people make when investing or how to hedge against market losses in a bad economy.

Those of you who are consultants with a cosmetic or skin care company might blog about what colors are best for which skin tones, and foods or other products that help slow down the aging process. Since cosmetics and skin care are primarily marketed to women, you could write about virtually any topic that traditionally appeals to women: money saving tips, spring cleaning tips, fashion, shopping or decorating for example.

The point here is that you are giving people helpful information in a way that makes you attractive. When people visit your blog looking for answers, you can begin to build a relationship with them. A nice feature of blogs is that people can sign up to receive updates, meaning each time you update your blog, they will automatically receive an email with your latest blog post.

While you should not hard sell your opportunity, you should include a line or two about your products or opportunity at the end of a blog post, or as a sidebar. At a minimum, you can include a link to your network marketing website somewhere on your blog's home page.

Video Blogs

A video blog (or vlog) is a blog that uses video instead of text. Vlogs are a great way to show your personality and how you relate to people. They have a feeling of immediacy that a traditional blog cannot match. Plus, many people prefer watching a video to reading.

Most laptop computers have a built-in video camera that makes recording and saving video to your hard drive easy and convenient. Many vloggers today are using cell phones, as the video capability on these devices has made great gains in recent years. The process of uploading your videos to YouTube and linking them to your vlog takes just a few simple steps. Like a traditional blog, a vlog will cost you virtually nothing aside from the purchase of simple video recording and editing software.

We recommend that you polish your speaking skills before attempting a vlog. You will need good camera presence and for most people this takes much practice. We recommend that you keep your vlogs short, no longer than a minute or so. That's long enough to convey a solid message and short enough to prevent the average Internet user from wandering away before you finish. Once you become an accomplished vlogger, you may naturally progress to longer videos.

Blogging Takes Time

A blog will cost you very little money. In fact, there are plenty of places on the Internet where you can set up a blog for free. (WordPress and Blogger are two of the more widely used and free platforms.)

The tradeoff is that while blogging is inexpensive, it also takes time to gain traction. And, it takes a lot of *your* time. You have to research and you have to write. It's a considerable investment, and you should consider this before you start. If you don't like to write, you do have the option of using content that already exists online—this is called "curating"—but, searching for that content also takes a lot of time.

Let's suppose that you will be using your blog for the primary purpose of generating leads for your network marketing business. You set up a blog on one of the free blogging platforms and you are ready to go.

Now, you need followers. You may be blogging for several weeks or more before you gain any type of following. Don't be discouraged. It's part of the process.

Spend some time reading and commenting on other blogs that are relative to yours. This will help you develop your own voice, so to speak. It will help you more clearly define your interests and your perspective. It will also help you gain an identity as other bloggers and blog readers come to know you.

You can also use a feature called a "trackback." Suppose you are reading Jane's blog. Her most recent update inspires you and you decide to write about her blog post on *your* blog. First, whenever you borrow thoughts or other material from a fellow blogger, you should include in your blog post a link to the one you are quoting. Next, you should include a trackback, which creates a comment on Jane's blog to let her know you have quoted her. It also provides a link to *your* blog, so Jane's readers can see what you have to say about what she said.

Other ways to build traffic to your blog:

1) Consider the title and description of your blog carefully. These will be indexed by the search engines and among the first things scanned when someone does a search. If you are writing primarily about nutritional supplements, consider using the words "nutritional supplements" in your title and description. This will enhance your search engine ranking.

2) Add your blog to your email signature line. Every time you send an email, the recipient will be exposed to a link to your blog.

3) Make regular updates. Determine a schedule—for instance, twice a week, once a week or every other week—and stick to it. People (and search engines) don't hold blogs in high regard when their content is seldom updated.

4) Interact with your readers. When you get a comment on your blog, acknowledge that you read it with a quick comment of your own. You'll increase the chance that people come back for more.

5) Submit your blog to search engines, directories and blog indices such as Technorati. Most of them will eventually find you, but by registering your blog you will be found more quickly.

6) Have social icons on your blog that connect to your Facebook profile (better yet, your fan page), your Twitter account, LinkedIn profile and any other social media accounts you have.

7) Your blog should also have a "share" feature, in which the reader can easily tell their friends about your blog through social media, email and other sources. You can do this easily with free widgets such as "Share This."

8) Become familiar with the Google Keyword Tool. It's a free, web-based search tool that will tell you how many people are searching using a particular keyword. For example, you can find out how many people are searching the phrase "best skin care." If you hit on a popular search term—"best skin care" was searched 74,000 times per month when we checked—use it in your blog post. However, don't abuse keywords. Using a phrase over and over indiscriminately is called "keyword stuffing" and can cause search engines to bury your blog or may even get you banned from search results. "In a 500-word post," says Joshua, "the general standard is to use the keyword or keyphrase in the title, introductory paragraph, once in the body, and once in the conclusion."

By the way, the search phrase "best skin care" is highly competitive, meaning a lot of people—probably hundreds—are already using it. As a result, it will take a lot of work and time (and perhaps money) for you to be able to capitalize on that particular phrase. You might research keywords more in depth to determine the best search optimization strategy for your needs.

Make It Your Own

The Internet is an easy place to steal things. With a few clicks of your mouse, you can copy large amounts of text, grab images and graphics and even download videos. But, just because you can do these things, it doesn't mean you should. Never copy another blogger's words, paste them into your blog post and try to pass them off as your own. This practice is called "scraping," and not only is it unethical, it is illegal. Curating is okay; scraping is not. If you want to use another blogger's material (or any material on the Internet for that matter), get permission first and then be sure to give proper credit. Bloggers love to have people comment on their blogs and appreciate the exposure you give them by linking to their blog when you repost what they have written. This may lead to you developing an ongoing relationship with that person, and who knows where that relationship might lead. Perhaps they will eventually look at your business or product.

The lesson here is that you need to be authentic. Remember that people follow people who are genuine and relatable. Don't pretend to be someone you aren't by scraping content from other places on the web. The Internet community is very good at identifying and exposing fakes; eventually it will catch up with you.

Your ultimate goal as a blogger is to build a community of followers that you communicate with regularly and who will come to regard you as a trusted expert. To do this, you must put in the hard work of generating at least some own original content. Keep it real; make it your own.

Social Media

Facebook is a star. It is a bona fide phenomenon that just keeps getting more and more phenomenal. With a recent growth curve that is nearly vertical, Facebook has rocketed into social orbit. Facebook was launched in 2004 and within two years had 12 million users.[6] That's pretty impressive. But it's nothing compared to what has happened since. By the end of 2011, Facebook had grown to 800 million users,[7] *a 67-fold increase in just five years!*

Is it any wonder that network marketers have jumped all over it? It's free, it's easy to use and hundreds of millions of people are using it!

Unfortunately, the way that most of us in this business use Facebook and the other social media is largely ineffective. In fact, we may even be hurting ourselves. Most of the time, we log on and essentially holler about how great our opportunity is and how awesome our products are. And, while our opportunity *is* great and our products *are* awesome, when we pepper our Facebook page constantly with salesy updates, "it just becomes noise," says social media trainer Mari Smith. "People tune it out."[8]

It's not just networkers, says Smith. Most business owners in general don't understand social media marketing. "They think that if you just pour out a lot of content, like making offers or talking about the business, the product features or whatever," she says, "that eventually somebody's going to click on their link." But, that strategy rarely works.

Take a look at the last 10 Facebook updates you made about your products or your business. How many people *other than your fellow network marketers* responded in some way? Moreover, how many of your last 100 updates brought you a new customer or a new distributor, or even a lead? Probably not many, if any.

We need to understand that the social media—Facebook, Twitter, LinkedIn, Google+, My Space and myriad others—are networks. Many of us are members of our local chamber of commerce and other business groups. We wouldn't go to one of these networking meetings, stand in the middle of the room and read press releases about our business, would we? Yet, that's essentially what most of us are doing on the social media circuit.

Smith teaches her clients to use a strategy she calls *relationship marketing*. "It needs to be about the relationships," she says. "We need to genuinely care about people and focus on connecting and building relationships." And, says Smith, social media just happens to be the perfect venue for relationship building. "It's an arena whereby a savvy marketer or savvy business person can establish themselves as an expert in health, finances or whatever it is they do," she says. "As people get to know them better in the online world, they become more inquisitive. It often leads to *What is it that you actually do?* which leads to the opportunity to go further with them."

Positioning yourself as an expert. Building relationships. It sounds a lot like the description of attraction marketing we gave you several pages back, doesn't it? It should be clear to you by now that however you market on the Internet, whether it's a website, blog or social media, the key is to build a following of people by helping them solve a problem or providing an answer to their question.

Smith says it can be as simple as finding useful tips on the web and passing them along. "Being a quality curator is one of the best uses of social media," she says. "You become a reliable source of quality information within your niche."

For instance, you might use an inspiring quote, a news item or an amazing statistic in your Facebook status updates or Twitter tweets. Keep it short and to the point. Then, provide a link to your blog or Facebook fan page where you give more information related to the quote, news item or statistic you just referenced. And—this is very important—you should also have information available on your products and business opportunity. "You still do have to put business content in there, a call to action or at least letting people know what you do," says Smith. "But, you can't make it 100 percent that. That's what makes it noise."

So, fellow networkers, let's all put away our megaphones and focus on building relationships. Remember that social networks are *networks* and you are in the *networking* business. Use social media to position yourself as a helpful expert, connect to people and develop a throng of followers. In time, they will come to trust you, many will buy from you and some will even join you.

Final Thoughts On Marketing

When it comes to marketing your business, you have many, many choices. We've outlined just a few of the tools for you, some of them free and some of them not, some of them simple and some of them not.

We cannot say this strongly enough: If you choose to advertise, do not jump into it blindly. Do your homework. Ask questions. Make informed decisions.

Unfortunately, when it comes to advertising, many network marketers get swept out with the tide. They see everybody else doing it and they think they need to be doing it, too. The problem is they are ill-prepared, lacking the grit, knowledge and financial resources to play the game.

When advertising doesn't work for them, they think the only thing to do is stay the course, to keep throwing more and more money into advertising. It's only a matter of time before they are frustrated and in serious debt.

Don't let this happen to you. Continuously evaluate your marketing efforts. If it's working, then run with it. Make hay while the sun shines. But, if it's not working—especially if you're paying handsomely for it—drop it. The sooner, the better.

There are plenty of ways to meet people that don't cost you any money; most of them begin with "Hello."

Consider, also, how your marketing efforts might impact duplication in your business. For instance, if you use a blog as a prospecting tool will your downline think they have to have one, too? If you are working exclusively in the cold market and spending hundreds of dollars a month, will your downline think they have to do the same? We learned from Randy Gage that when we make the business look difficult and complicated, it becomes unduplicatable. You should give this serious thought when planning your marketing.

Finally, remember that nothing is more important than the person you are talking to. Nothing can replace relationships. Tools are just tools; marketing is just marketing. This will always be a business of investing in people, one relationship at a time.

Quick Review: Harnessing The Internet

1) Don't ignore the Internet. Your prospects *expect* you to have an online presence.
2) The Internet is convenient and a huge time saver. But, it is also unregulated. Expect a lot of negative misinformation about the industry and your company.
3) Most network marketing websites are designed as presentation tools, not prospecting tools. Don't expect your website to do something it isn't designed to do.
4) Attraction marketing can work effectively in your business, particularly if you have a blog.
5) When using blogs and social media, don't hit people over the head with your network marketing hammer. A softer sell is better.
6) Marketing tools are just tools. Relationships are what matter.

Exercise

1) What information could you provide to your prospects that would make you more attractive to them? If you were to start a blog, what would you write about?

TWELVE

Back To The Dream

At the beginning of this book, we gave you a seminal challenge: to figure out what you want out of this business, to define your WHY. We feel so strongly about this that we instructed you to stop and give it serious thought before you continued reading the book. We sincerely hope you have done that.

Your WHY is your rudder; it gives you direction. It is the wind in your sails, propelling you forward. It is your anchor, holding you fast in the storm.

Before we send you on your way, we are going to revisit the Dream. In these last few pages, we want to inspire you with a few more stories and give you a healthy dose of encouragement.

We All Arrive At The Same Place

In Chapter 1, we introduced you to Doris Lessing, who had extraordinary needs that kept her on the run, day and night. She was faced with the sudden loss of her husband, the specter of raising her kids alone and having to earn a living after being out of the workforce for many years.

When we are faced with extreme circumstances like Doris was, it is nearly impossible to think about anything else, isn't it? There is that rare person who, despite their hardships, says, "I saw the big picture right from the beginning." But, most of us don't think that far ahead. We can't see past our dire straits.

This type of short-sightedness can actually work to your advantage in the beginning; when you are about to lose your house, you tend to be focused and highly motivated. But, an urgent need is a relatively short-term motivation. Once you get that solution, where do you go from there?

Within a few years, Doris' income had exceeded $100,000 a year. For the first time in a long time, life became comfortable. She met Henry Leissing and in 2001 they were married. Her six-figure income doubled, then tripled, then quadrupled. Today, Doris and Henry live in a spacious home in the mountains in Flat Rock, North Carolina. Life is good, very good.

But, along the way Doris came to a juncture in her business, a place where her WHY had to change. With no urgent need nipping at her heels, there was nothing for her to run from. Instead, she had to set her sights on something to run *to*. That something was her Dream:

> To be able to have some financial freedom now, in my retirement years, to provide opportunities for my children and grandchildren, to live life according to my values and purpose in life, means so much to me. I am so glad that I did not let my initial fears and insecurities get the best of me, and that I kept my mind and heart open to explore this industry.
>
> During the five years that I built the business as a single mom, I sent my daughter to college and paid for her education, bought a home, cared for my mother, and expanded my business nationally and internationally. By the time I remarried, my income was already exceeding a quarter of a million dollars a year. That still stuns me. I grew up in very modest circumstances, and despite the fact that I have both an undergraduate and graduate school education, our work in ministry had always kept our income very minimal.
>
> I believe that, truly, network marketing is a ground floor opportunity that can provide the means for people with a strong work ethic to pull themselves out of marginal circumstances and to flourish in the marketplace and in the world. It is an opportunity to use one's talents and gifts on behalf of others. And since there is nobody to tell you when to retire, you can continue to work as long as you wish, and have a positive impact on others as long as you live.
>
> I thank God every day for the amazing gift this has been to our family. It has been almost 20 years, and I am still deeply committed to my business partners, to our company, and to the culture within which we serve.

Eventually, we all arrive at the same place: the pursuit of a Dream. If you think about it, building a network marketing business is a very elegant process: it helps us identify that we have a Dream, it gives us hope that we can achieve that Dream, it produces tremendous personal growth as we pursue the Dream, and it provides a business model that can deliver the Dream!

In Chapter 2, we told you the story of Charlie Emmenecker, who had worked in the golf industry. His wife, Nancy, spent many years in the corporate marketplace. They have left those careers behind, thanks to their network marketing business, and now live very comfortably. It's interesting that Charlie's goals for his network marketing business were initially pretty modest. That changed quickly:

> In the beginning, my Dream was to make three to four thousand dollars a month to go along with my golf business. I thought that would be pretty cool. Well, it wasn't very long—it was only three to four months—before we were there and had achieved that income goal. So, the Dream got bigger.
>
> We kept our heads down and kept working. Five years went by. One day the corporate office called to tell us that we were to be inducted into the Million Dollar Earner Hall of Fame. I was surprised, because we hadn't been counting dollars; we hadn't been focused on the money. I knew it would be there if we did what we needed to do. But, after that call I did some calculations and figured out that we had actually made $1.3 million in our first five years.
>
> We pulled out the dream board and there it was: our future home. While we were building the business, Nancy had cut out a picture from a brochure and put it on the board. This was her dream home.
>
> Two years into our business, we were able to buy the land. In 2008, the house was completed and we moved in. It's 5,300 square feet and has been valued at nearly $1 million. A lot of people thought it was crazy to build that big of a house in northwest Ohio. But, it's our dream home.
>
> It has also helped our business. People come from all over to be trained here. They stay here with us. We've had the opportunity to make a lot of friends and strengthen the bonds we have with the people in our group.

I encourage people to not be afraid to expand their Dream as things begin to materialize in their business. Thoughts are things; a Dream can become reality. Nancy cut a picture out of a brochure, put it on the dream board and we built that *exact* house. And, we show people that.

From here forward, we're just continuing to live the Dream. We have plans to travel; we want to see the rest of the world. And, we know our check will be there. Every month, it goes *ping!* into our checking account.

Your Dream Has No Expiration Date

In 1963, archaeologists were working an excavation site at Masada, an ancient seaside fortress built by King Herod, when they unearthed a cache of seeds. It was later determined that the seeds were from a date palm, a long-extinct species, no less. Carbon dating revealed that the seeds were 2,000 years old.

Checking historical records, researchers concluded that the seeds had likely been left there by Jewish rebels who had commandeered the fortress while fighting for freedom from Roman rule. Some 900 Jews died at Masada in AD 73 when the Roman army closed in on them. The story of Masada is famous among the Jewish people, symbolizing their determination to be free in their own land.

After being discovered, the seeds were kept in an office desk drawer for another 40 years. But in 2005, Israeli scientists planted some of them and, to the amazement of the world…produced a seedling![1] *A seed that is two thousand years old and from an extinct species…PRODUCED LIFE!*

Do you see the incredible symbolism in that? Take a moment to soak it in. Maybe you had a Dream once upon a time, but it has been buried for years. Maybe you are frustrated because your business isn't growing and you're afraid it has no life left in it. Maybe the entire struggle has left you cynical; to you, a Dream is simply an extinct notion.

For more than 2,000 years, that seed endured. It waited. And, it waited. Once unearthed, it was put in a drawer and had to wait another 40 years! Has that happened to you? Maybe you waited for what seemed like forever, then got your chance—you were as giddy as a child on Christmas morning—only to be put in a drawer once again. It's enough to make you wonder if your Dream is really worth it. Maybe you've been knocked down so many times you're not sure how to get up any more.

This remarkable palm tree, named Methuselah, is now six years old and four and a half feet tall. In November of 2011 it was planted in a visitor's park at an Israeli research university, where it is now on display for the world to see.[2]

Whatever discouragement, doubt or hesitation you might be feeling, take heart. The seeds of a Dream never die. There is no expiration date on your success!

Yes, life is hard—cruel, at times. But, nothing in this life can kill your Dream. Your Dream is not extinct. You can still become what you were created to become. You can still have what you were created to have.

You can do this. We believe in you, and we want you to dream again.

The happiest, most fulfilled and most successful people on earth are the ones who chase their Dream. They go for it and they never stop.

Don't wait another day.

Follow your heart. Chase your Dream!

About The Authors

Dave Bradley

Dave Bradley was born and raised in Manchester, England. Dave is highly experienced when it comes to dealing with people in the business and sporting world.

He was a professional soccer player for more than 10 years, playing for Manchester United and Doncaster Rovers in England. He also played for Hellenic and Witz University in South Africa, and played and coached for Dunedin City and Manurewa FC in New Zealand.

Prior to starting his own network business, Dave was an insurance agent for five years with Australian Mutual Provident in New Zealand.

In 1987, Dave started his network marketing business with the hope of becoming financially independent. By 1992, he was able to set up a residual income that allowed him to pursue his dream of helping others achieve the success they want.

Due to considerable success in his business, Dave was given the opportunity to travel the world mentoring business leaders and as a motivational speaker. Some of the countries include the United States, Canada, Australia, South Africa, England, Belgium, Holland, Hong Kong and New Zealand.

After 20 years of living in New Zealand, where he met his wife, Melony, they moved to her home town of Maumee, Ohio USA, with two of their children, Olivia and Mackenzie. Dave's son, Andrew, lives in Manchester, England.

Dave has a strong interest in health and wellness and lives that out on a daily basis. He has a passion for leadership, people and personal development.

He is a family man and prides himself on being the best husband, father and brother he can be. Dave is a committed Christian and attends www.thechurchonstrayer.com in Maumee, Ohio. The pastor is Dave's father-in-law, Tony Scott.

Dave would like to dedicate his involvement in the co-writing of this book to his mother, Marjorie, who lives in England and his late father, Graham, who died at age 48.

Rodney Brandt

Rodney Brandt is a native of Defiance, Ohio, USA and the youngest of six children. He has worked in marketing and public relations since 1985 and in network marketing since 2001. His professional background also includes administrative-level experience in intercollegiate athletics and child welfare. Rod is a published writer and frequent seminar presenter. He and his wife, Lori, are co-owners of Covenant Marketing Services, LLC (http://covenantmarketingservices.com).

They have two children, Amanda and Cameron, and live in Maumee, Ohio, USA. Rod is passionate about his Christian faith, business, missions and his own personal development.

Acknowledgements

First and foremost, we thank God for His love, provision and inspiration. All good things in this life are from His hand.

To our wives, Melony and Lori: thank you for being our sounding board when we needed to know if our ideas made sense. Thank you for your encouragement when we thought we would never finish the writing. Without you, this book would still be something Dave and Rod intend to do some day.

Thank you, Julie Ziglar Norman, for your wisdom, generosity and friendship. You have opened many doors for us and we are grateful.

To Doris Leissing, Charlie Emmenecker, Donna Reid-Mitchell, Ginny Fiscella and Randy Gage: thank you for lending us your experiences, knowledge and wisdom. Your stories bring our concepts to life.

To Mari Smith and Michael Lee Joshua: we're indebted to you for your expertise and your eagerness to teach us. Thank you for helping us make sense of the online world.

Thank you, Tiffany Colter, for being an outstanding publisher and a great friend, and for putting up with a thousand questions.

Resources

Chapter 1

1. *Up In The Air*, Paramount Pictures, 2009

2. Stephen R. Covey, *The 7 Habits of Highly Effective People: Powerful Lessons in Personal Change*, Revised Edition (Free Press: 2004), p.98

3. Joe Light, *More Workers Start To Quit*, The Wall Street Journal, May 25, 2010
http://online.wsj.com/article/
SB10001424052748704113504575264432377146698.html
Retrieved May 13, 2011

4. *Americans Hate Their Jobs More Than Ever*, MSNBC.com, February 26, 2007
http://www.msnbc.msn.com/id/17348695/ns/business-careers/t/americans-hate-their-jobs-more-ever/
Retrieved May 27, 2011

Chapter 2

1. World Federation of Direct Selling Associations, World Report on Product Categories – 2010
http://www.wfdsa.org/files/pdf/global-stats/
Product_Categories_Report_11311.pdf
Retrieved November 5, 2011

2. World Federation of Direct Selling Associations Statistics
http://www.wfdsa.org/library/?fa=statistical_information
Retrieved July 20, 2011

3. World Federation of Direct Selling Associations, Global Statistical Report – 2010
http://www.wfdsa.org/files/pdf/global-stats/
Global_Statistical_Report_11311.pdf
Retrieved November 5, 2011

4. World Federation of Direct Selling Associations Statistics
http://www.wfdsa.org/library/?fa=statistical_information
Retrieved July 20, 2011

5. Direct Selling Offers Flexibility and Financial Freedom, *Success Magazine*, May 5, 2008

6. Debra Valentine, *Pyramid Schemes,* speech presented at the International Monetary Fund's Seminar On Current Legal Issues Affecting Central Banks, 1998
http://www.ftc.gov/speeches/other/dvimf16.shtm
Retrieved July 21, 2011

7. Chris Widener, *The Invisible Profit System*, Audio CD (Chris Widener: 2007)

8. Entrepreneur.com, *McDonald's*
http://www.entrepreneur.com/franchises/mcdonalds/282570-0.html
Retrieved April 21, 2010

9. CNN Money, *How Much It Takes To Start A Business*, 2006
http://money.cnn.com/2006/08/17/smbusiness/wells_fargo_study/index.htm
Retrieved April 26, 2010

10. Forbes.com, *Top-Earning Dead Celebrities*, Oct. 25, 2010
http://www.forbes.com/2010/10/21/michael-jackson-elvis-presley-tolkien-business-entertainment-dead-celebs-10-intro.html
Retrieved November 14, 2010

Chapter 3

1. Tyler H. McCormick, Matthew J. Salganik, Tian Zheng (2010), *How Many People Do You Know?: Efficiently Estimating Personal Network Size*, Journal of the American Statistical Association 105:489, 59-70

Chapter 8

1. Enjoying Everyday Life (Joyce Meyer Ministries), *I Am Relentless, Part 2* television show, Feb. 9, 2010

2. *The Holy Bible,* Proverbs 12:1 (TLB)

Chapter 9

1. Daniel Gross, *Forbes Greatest Business Stories Of All Time* (Wiley: 1997), p. 86-88

2. Jesus Christ, *The Holy Bible,* Luke 15:11-32 (NLT)

Chapter 11

1. Pingdom, *Internet 2011 In Numbers* blog post
http://royal.pingdom.com/2012/01/17/internet-2011-in-numbers/ (The number
of websites added in 2011 and annually was also taken from this source.)
Retrieved January 22, 2012

2. All Michael Lee Joshua quotes are from email correspondence, December 1, 2011.
You can find Michael Lee Joshua at http://paynopostage.com.

3. *Search, Display Trends Push Online Ad Spend Past $31 Billion*, eMarketer.com, July
5, 2011.
http://www.emarketer.com/Article.aspx?R=1008476
Retrieved November 7, 2011

4. *Consolidation of Online Ad Market Continues as Google Grabs More Share,*
eMarketer.com, June 21, 2011
http://www.emarketer.com/Article.aspx?R=1008452
Retrieved November 7, 2011

5. David Meerman Scott, *Developing Thought Leadership Content* blog post
http://www.davidmeermanscott.com/thought_leadership02.htm
Retrieved May 9, 2011

6. *Facebook Facts & Figures (history & statistics)*, Website Monitoring Blog
http://www.website-monitoring.com/blog/2010/03/17/facebook-facts-and-
figures-history-statistics/
Retrieved May 10, 2011

7. Facebook corporate website
http://www.facebook.com/press/info.php?statistics
Retrieved December 1, 2011

8. All Mari Smith quotes are from a one-on-one interview via Skype, November 21,
2011. You can find Mari Smith at http://marismith.com.

Chapter 12

1. *2,000-Year-Old Seed Sprouts, Sapling Is Thriving*, National Geographic News,
November 22, 2005
http://news.nationalgeographic.com/news/2005/11/1122_051122_old_seed.html
Retrieved January 8, 2012

2. email correspondence from Abby Lutman, Arava Institute for Environmental
Studies, Kibbutz Ketura, Israel; January 8, 2012

www.ingramcontent.com/pod-product-compliance
Lightning Source LLC
Chambersburg PA
CBHW031928190326
41519CB00007B/446